Unleash Your Inner Greatness

Guide to overcoming obstacles and tapping into the person you were always meant to be.

By

Dr. Donavan L. Outten

Walk in Faith! You got this....

Cover design by:
Designs by Manh Tuan

Editing by:
Vernetta K. Williams, Ph.D.
Chrysalis Consulting

Text Layout & Format Assistance by:
Cynthia D. Johnson –
www.diverseskillscenter.com

Printed in the United States of America
ISBN: 978-1499509687

Contents

Dedication

This book is dedicated to every fighter who feels that they have lost a round in life, but had the audacity to get back up and fight again because they believe that they are in the will of God. It is never too late to stand up and claim what is yours.

Acknowledgements

First and foremost, I would like to thank my Lord and Savior Jesus Christ who is the head of my life. Thank you for giving me the strength, the will and endurance to complete this book. For everyone who contributed to this book I want to say thank you for letting me tell your amazing story of strength, courage and bravery of turning your setback into a comeback.

I am eternally grateful to my family and friends who have supported me over the years; you are my foundation. Thank you "Pops" up in heaven watching over me I hope that I am making you proud. Love you Man!

Introduction

Greatness is in every human being, but how do you tap into that greatness when your back is against the wall, when you are hurt, when you are broken, or when the odds are stacked against you? *Unleash your Inner Greatness* is a guide to help individuals overcome obstacles they may be facing in their life.

It is a tough task to wake up every day and face the world and the problems that are thrown against you. Every time you seem like you're getting ahead or just settling into your own, something comes up and throws you off track. You find yourself wondering how you are going to make it through another day; how are you going to make it through another week; how are you going to make it through this situation?

You are fighting a constant battle, and you are not alone in this struggle. Many people are fighting the same battle as you are. The key is not how to win the battle; it is how to win the war. Before you can fight any battle you have to mentally prepare yourself for the battle. You have to know your enemy, who you are fighting, why you are fighting, and what you are willing to sacrifice in battle to win this war? You have to first visualize in your mind what you want to accomplish, because this battle will test every fiber of your being. What is it in life that you are fighting for that the enemy does not want you to have? What are you willing to do or give up in order to go after your dreams and fulfill your destiny?

Some of the most important questions you have to ask yourself are, "Where am I today in my life? Am I a happy person? What do I really want out of life? Am I living the life I thought I was going to live?" Be totally honest with yourself and where you are today; look at yourself in the mirror and at your life as you know it. Then decide, am I ready for a change? Am I ready to be better today than I was yesterday? Am I ready for greatness?

This book provides thought provoking concepts that allow you to work through challenges if your life. The "Bring-it-Home" sections of the book provide practical applications that anyone can do. It is designed to push you forward and get you out of your comfort zone to become better. The "Get-it-Together" section challenges you to take your life or situation to the next level. You can no longer make excuses but prepare yourself for greatness.

Unleash your Inner Greatness has many biblical references throughout the book and talks about God and the impact that God can make in your life. However, the book also references that you should believe in a higher power even if your religion is something else other than Christianity. The end goal is the same; get out of your own way and become what

you were destined to become, and that is
GREAT!

Resilience

Fall seven times, Stand up eight

*"Our greatest glory is not in never falling, but in rising
every time we fall."*

- Confucius

*"My resilience comes from wanting to be a happy person -
everything I do is always about trying to find a solution."*

- Dan O'Brien

Lance Armstrong reached the pinnacle of international road racing cycling only after overcoming a near-fatal case of cancer. Suffering from chronic pain, Lance was diagnosed with testicular cancer that eventually spread to his lungs and brain. With chances of recovery less than 50%, Lance began a course of treatment that included two surgeries and chemotherapy. With time, the treatment began to work, and Lance was on his way to a full recovery.

The chemotherapy took a toll on Lance's body, so he was left feeling weak and fragile. Remarkably, just five months after his initial diagnosis, Lance was back on a bike rebuilding the strength he had lost. Not only did the cancer take its toll on Lance physically, but the emotional impact was traumatic as well. Most people who discover that they have cancer go through a sense of loss and hopelessness. Nothing makes you stand up and take stock of your life like a cancer diagnosis. After undergoing surgery and intensive chemotherapy treatments for testicular cancer, he returned to training and, in 1999, became only the second American to win the Tour de France.

In 2005, Lance won the Tour de France for the seventh straight time, holding the record for the most Tour victories in history. While Armstrong's record is impressive, and that was not the surprising part, he accomplished all of this after undergoing brain and testicular surgery as well as extensive chemotherapy to treat testicular cancer that metastasized to his brain and lungs in 1996. Armstrong's passion for riding and resilience is what helped him overcome his battle with cancer and got him back on that bike to become the great champion that he is today.

Although Lance Armstrong admitted to taking steroids, I argue that his will and skills allowed him to win the Tour de France, not the drugs. In no way do I support the use of performance enhancing drugs; I do believe, though, that the winner mentality was innate in him. While the drug may make you stronger, it does not make you smarter, it does not give you the desire to push past the pain, nor does it give you the will to win. The Will to Win comes from the inside.

The path toward nurturing a resilient mindset and lifestyle is a road that should not be taken lightly. This path has many bumps, twists, turns, and pot-holes and is never straightforward. The road often contains obstacles and detours that interfere with reaching your destination. However, the more knowledgeable you are about the components of a resilient mindset, as well as the roadblocks to its success, the more conscientious you can become to change any existing counter-productive ways of thinking, feeling, and behaving. By so doing, you become better equipped and confident to discover those paths that lead to a productive, fulfilling life, a life that encourages you to plan and dream, to bring joy to others, to laugh, and to appreciate that you truly are the person responsible for your own life.

Resilience is one of the most important emotional intelligence competencies you can have in today's fast-changing world. Emotional intelligence is the ability to identify, assess, and control the emotions of oneself, of others, and of groups. It means being able to bounce back after setbacks, failures, disappointments, and losses. It means not giving up and continuing to face the future with optimism and courage despite events. In tough times, resilient people do not give up. They face their stress directly, learn from the past, and reach out for and use resources. They also reinterpret negative meanings into positive ones.

Resilient people consistently choose an optimistic outlook on life. An optimistic attitude is one of hopeful expectation for positive results. It is also flexible because a flexibly optimistic viewpoint does not discount the negative events of life, but intentionally and realistically looks for the best outcome in any situation. It is this "looking for the best" that pulls resilient people through hard times and pulls them back into shape. A positive attitude reduces the potential for stress and depression.

Most resilient people enjoy life by making the intentional choice to participate in it. Resilient people accept the fact that on some days they don't "feel" like going to work, cleaning the house, or attending a party. However, they also know that it is important to do these things whether or not they feel like it. Like motivational speaker Les Brown says, "In order to get what you don't have, you must be willing to do what you haven't done." Don't be afraid of the unknown. Go out there and make it happen; if you happen to fail, let failure be your teacher.

Bounce Back

It is a tough task to wake up every day and face the world and the problems thrown against you. Every time it seems like you're getting ahead or just settling into your own, something comes up and throws you off track. You find yourself wondering how you are going to make it through another day; how are you going to make it through another week; how are you going to make it through this situation. You are fighting a constant battle. I know you often ask, "How do I Bounce Back?"

Well, you are not alone in this fight! Many people are fighting the same battle that you are fighting. The key is not how to win the battle; it is how to win the war. Before you can fight any battle, you have to mentally prepare yourself for the battle. You have to know your enemy, who you are fighting, why you are fighting, and what you are willing to sacrifice during the battle to win this war. You have to first visualize in your mind what you want to accomplish because this battle will test every fiber of your being.

Compare this situation to professional athletes who train every day to be at the top of their profession. They watch game film of their competitors, go to the gym 4-5 hours a day, practice 4-5 days a week, and still may lose the battle in competition. Enough losses could result in being cut from the team, loss of contract, loss of income, and end of career.

The one key ingredient I have found in people who know how to bounce back from a bad situation is they know how to *"reinvent themselves."* In life, you are guaranteed to be dealt bad situations. As long as you are breathing, you and no other person on the Earth will live an exclusively charmed life. If you are able to take that situation and learn from it, dissect it, digest it, accept it for what it is at that moment, and move on, then you can reinvent yourself into something greater, something stronger, and something wiser. This may be the time to change careers, go back to school, open a business, find a new love, or start a new life!

What is it in life that you are fighting for that the enemy does not want you to have? What are you willing to do or to give up, in order to go after your dreams and fulfill your destiny?

Learn to Deal with Mistakes

The ways in which we understand and respond to mistakes and failure are an integral part of a resilient mindset. When you make a mistake, what do you tell yourself? How do you react? Resilient people consider mistakes as experiences for learning and growth. They ask themselves, "What can I do differently next time in order to succeed?" Those who are not resilient typically interpret mistakes as attributable to conditions that cannot be easily corrected, such as a lack of intelligence. They feel defeated by mistakes and often end up blaming others, quitting, or refusing to attempt things.

Observe what you say to yourself when you make a mistake. It will give you a clue to how resilient you are and what you might have to change. Use this exercise to help you recognize the change in yourself.

What was the last mistake that I made?

_____
_____
_____

How did I react?

_____
_____
_____

What did I learn from my mistake?

_____
_____
_____

What will I do differently next time?

_____
_____
_____

Strategies for Resilience

When challenged or distressed, resilient people expect to find a way to make things work well. They feel capable and self-reliant. Here are some strategies to becoming resilient:

- Find meaning and purpose in your struggles.
- Know when you need help and get it.
- Face reality head-on, labeling your setbacks, losses, and disappointments for what they are.
- Reinterpret negative meanings into positive ones.
- Determination, patience, and courage are the only things needed to improve any situation.
- Knowing is not enough. You must be willing to give and sacrifice 100%.

Bringing It Home

1. Work On Being Optimistic and Hopeful
It may seem counter-intuitive to adopt an optimistic outlook when you're feeling down, but research indicates that people can "try on" new ways of seeing things. Start telling yourself that things will work out somehow if you try your best. Once again, you may not believe it at first, but experimenting with being hopeful won't hurt. This is especially true when you are engaged in a frustrating situation.

2. Stick To It
Practice sticking to a task or project. Persistence is important when cultivating resilience.
Refusing to give up makes it more likely that you will overcome obstacles. If you know you can make a commitment, see it through and celebrate your achievements. The next time your job sends you a curve ball, you'll know you have the fortitude to deal with it.

3. Think About the Worst And Plan For It
If you suffer a financial setback, how are you going to handle it? What is your back-up plan? Do you have enough money to live on for six months if you should lose your job? Be prepared to deal with adversities. Life has a way of interfering with our goals. We can't anticipate all of the difficulties we may face, but we can plan for some of the more frightening ones.

Thoughts

God will allow pain to teach you what pride wouldn't let you learn. But you have to fight through the pain, through the heartache, and through the storm. Every day was not promised to be sunny, but every day was not promised to be rainy either. Once you have weathered the storm and gone through what you needed to go through, then your blessing will come. In fact, you won't even have to deal with these things along, for God promises to be with you through difficulties: "When you pass through waters, I will be with you. When you cross rivers, you will not drown. When you walk through fire, you will not be burned, nor will the flames hurt you. This is because I, the Lord, am your God, the Holy One of Israel, your Savior." Isaiah 43: 2-3

Get-It-Together

Some of the most important questions you have to ask yourself are, "Where am I today in my life? Am I a happy person? What do I really want out of life? Am I living the life I thought I was going to live?" Be totally honest with yourself and where you are today; look at yourself in the mirror and ask yourself, "Am I resilient enough to bounce back and live the life that I deserve?" I challenge you to write these questions down and answer them honestly. If you don't like the answers on that piece of paper, then let's develop a plan to make changes in your life.

Determination

You must pay the price if you wish to secure the blessing

"Keep your dreams alive. Understand to achieve anything requires faith and belief in yourself, vision, hard work, determination, and dedication. Remember all things are possible for those who believe".

-Gail Devers

"You have to learn the rules of the game. And then you have to play better than anyone else."

- Albert Einstein

Where does the power of determination come from? How does an individual muster up enough strength to have such strong determination to finish a task or overcome a devastating life situation? Where do they find the courage to stand up for what they believe in or battle back from a medical condition that almost took their life? How does one leave a secure job to start a business that they are passionate about? What is the secret to obtaining determination and maintaining it over a period of time? What kinds of people have it, and what is determination?

In my heart, I truly believe that determination is having the will to move forward in spite of what obstacle, barrier, or difficulty you might be facing. It is looking adversity in the face and not backing down, but pushing forward with tenacity. Self-determination starts on the inside. It is first a thought or a belief that you can or will succeed no matter the problem you have to face. You believe in yourself even when no one else does. That spells confidence, character, and courage.

Determination and motivation constitute critical factors in how far an individual will develop. Intense drive and determination may be the most distinguishing characteristics of a successful person who will rise to the top. We are surrounded by determined people every day but rarely realize it because we are living in our own world and don't recognize the world around us. Sometimes, people's mistakes end up being their blessings later in life when they are determined to succeed.

Jamie and Nicole were high school sweethearts, but in the midst of the high school romance, they had a child, Jalen, when they were 14 years old. With the support of their family, they continued and finished high school. Nicole graduated with honors.

Jamie, wanting to be near his family, gave up his football scholarship and went to the same college as Nicole so that they could raise their son. During their freshman year, Nicole got pregnant again with their second child, but that did not stop them from obtaining their education. Four years later, they both graduated with Bachelor's degrees from the University of South Florida because they were determined to have a better life for their family. Currently, Nicole is a Physician Assistant, and Jamie owns his own business. They are married with four children. Ironically, Jalen attended Pace University on a football scholarship 18 years after Jamie gave up his football scholarship to care for his son, Jalen, when he was born.

The will of God will never take you where the grace of God will not protect you. If you are in the will of God, you are always protected. So, you should have no fear. Be relentless toward achieving your goals and defying the impossible. Adam T. was a star athlete and a defensive back for a Division One college program. With less than two minutes left in a game against Ohio

State, the Ohio State's football team held a commanding 45-6 lead and was running out the clock. The ball was snapped and handed off to a 231-pound running back. On the other side, freshman defensive back Adam T., 18, saw that the play, an end sweep, was coming right at him.

"I knew he was a big back, so I decided that I was going to take his legs," Adam T. remembers the game last fall. "He was running at a slow pace, and then he sped up. My head was at the wrong place at the wrong time. His knee hit the top of my helmet and snapped my head downward and then, darkness."

Two days after the accident, Adam had spinal fusion surgery. The prognosis was grim. One doctor told Adam T.'s father that the chance his son would walk again was 3 in 100. Adam never heard those odds. He knew he was badly hurt but never considered not walking again.

Because of Adam's determination and great medical attention, he went from being paralyzed to walking again. With intense physical therapy and the will to walk again, Adam believed in himself and was able to defy the impossible. Although he would never play football again, he regained a certain quality of life that is immeasurable, the ability to walk with his own power like he did before the accident.

Determination comes in all forms from amazing sports recoveries to individuals who were unemployed for 5 years. Jessica H. was a successful Pharmaceutical Sales Representative for 10 years making more than $100,000 before she got pregnant. She decided to be a stay-at-home mom until her child was elementary school aged. When her child was 5 years old and Jessica started to look for work, no one would hire her. The 5-year gap in employment proved to be a barrier for her when seeking employment.

Jessica remembers counting the rejections from employers, and at year four, they were more than 1,000. Feeling penalized for wanting to be a good mom who spent time with her daughter she almost gave up, but she pressed even harder. Jessica wanted to stay in her industry because she was good at it and had a passion for it. On a Tuesday morning while at her computer, the phone rang, and it was the call she had been waiting for. It took 5 long years of putting in applications before she got the job that she wanted. While Jessica may have been deterred for a moment, she was not defeated, and her determination paid off.

Determination equals Successful People

Successful people want to win, to achieve, and to excel. However, individuals with self-motivation and drive go after their goals with an unwavering intention that separates them from others.

Successful people typically have a high level of self-confidence. They know what they want out of life. They know how to use their strengths to reach their goals. They tend to take more risks, and they are not afraid of failure. Overall, there is something about the nature of the beliefs that peak performers have that builds confidence and spurs motivation. They hold beliefs that further and support their goals. They adopt beliefs which are consistent with their achieving success and high-level performance.

The level and strength of motivation has a direct impact on how well a successful person will persevere through rigorous times, setbacks, possible injuries, and disappointments. With self-determination, the successful people persevere and remain unwavering in their focus on goals.

Eric Thomas, "The Hip Hop Preacher," told a story about a young man who wanted to be successful, so he sought help from a guru. The guru told the young man to meet him at 4am at the beach. The young man said, "I want to make money; I don't want to learn how to swim." The guru replied, "If you want to learn how to make money and be successful, meet me at 4am." So, the young man arrived at the beach at 4am in a suit and ready to learn.

The guru took the young man by the hand and walked him out to the water waist deep and then until the water was at the young man's shoulders. The guru took the young man by the neck and held his head under water. The young man started scratching, clawing, and whaling his arms under the water trying to get to the surface to breathe. Just before he was about to pass out, the guru let him up. The guru asked the young man a question, "When you were under water, what did you want to do?" The young man said, "I wanted to breathe!"

The guru looked the young man in the eyes and said, "When you want to succeed as badly as you wanted to breathe, then you will be successful." Your self-determination should force you to get out of your comfort zone and go beyond your ability to succeed.

Staying Steadfast and Focused

There is something going on in your life right now that you are going through no matter how big or small it might be. Nonetheless, you are being challenged. Choose a problem or project that you would like to improve in your life right now. Tell yourself, "I am not going to wait another day and let it linger." You are going to be determined to get results, so use the following exercise to start the process:

1. *Acknowledge the Problem*: Write down in detail exactly what the problem or project is that is hindering your life.

_____

_____

_____

2. *Solution A*: Write down what you think is an obvious solution to the problem.

_____
_____
_____

3. *Solution B*: Write down what you think is an alternative solution to the problem.

_____
_____
_____

4. *Collaboration*: How can you make these two solutions work together to solve your problem?

_____
_____
_____

5. *Trust*: Once you have come up with a solution that you feel comfortable with, take the idea to people whom you trust. Select three people and listen closely to each of their responses. If you trust and respect them, you will value their input and insight into your situation. Also, look to people who have expertise or experience; people who have gone through your situation and can give you great and valuable information. People who are experts in their respective fields have vast amounts of knowledge, and you can learn from them.

If you are determined to get results, you will seek out the answers that you are looking for. Make this a practice with every situation that you encounter, and learn from your experiences so that you may grow from them and not resent them.

Bringing It Home

1. From Stumbling Blocks to Stepping Stones
In life, it is inevitable that you will encounter stumbling blocks along the way. You can't run, hide, or mislead them. Life will be challenging at times, and you will have to work for what you want to keep, have lost, or want to gain. But in the midst of those stumbling blocks, you have to find those stepping stones to your greatness. Life is truly about balance. For every low, there is a high. You have to go through those low and rough days and pay your dues in order to step into your high days of prosperity and greatness.

2. You have to be Determined to Change
According to leadership expert John C. Maxwell, "Positive expectations bring a positive attitude. They produce excitement, conviction, desire, confidence, commitment, and energy, all characteristics that help a person to achieve success. If you would like to possess these qualities in greater abundance, then raise your expectations." You have to be willing to change

your life if you want a better life. Success breeds success, so start socializing with successful people. Place yourself in situations where you can be successful and be committed to it.

3. *Be Determined to get Your Blessing*
Sometimes, your deliverance is not in what you do; it is in what you say. It is important to be mentally strong as well as physically strong. You have to be consistently positive in your thoughts to make a positive change in your life.

- Whatever you say, your mind supports.
- You cannot say in the midst of a storm, "I'm not going to make it."
- Your process will not silence your promise.
- Positive affirmations will help you through tough times.

Thoughts

No one can make you self-determined, and no one can make you happy, proud, or confident if you don't have these inner feelings already inside you. These are all personal attributes that each person must develop and define as a part of their own character. There are many people who are battling cancer, but they are determined to beat it and recover. There are people who have lost a limb, but they obtain a prosthetic and are living a quality life. There are people who have lost cars, jobs, homes, family members, but they are determined to keep living and striving for a better life. What are you determined to do? Make up your mind and heart to overcome any situation that falls at your feet then step over it.

Get-It-Together

The journey of life will test you; at certain times, the journey will try to break you. It is important that you have some kind of a *Spiritual Life.* Your *Spiritual Life* is more uplifting; it goes to the core of the soul. Your *Spiritual Life* believes in a higher power, the power that gets you through tough times. For many, your *Spiritual Life* believes that there is life after death and that higher power is God Almighty. Your *Spiritual Life* guides you through healing, faith, obedience, and the ability to forgive. God has a way of working even when we don't see Him working, but with prayer and faith, your journey will be less painful. Do not give up the fight! The quickest way to get God to help you is to put your knees on the floor and pray.

Develop a Clear Strategy

Putting your Life Plan in place is the first step to success

"It takes a lot of courage to release the familiar and seemingly secure, to embrace the new. But there is no real security in what is no longer meaningful. There is more security in the adventurous and exciting, for in movement there is life, and in change there is power."

-Alan Cohen

Are you tired of losing? How long has it been since you felt like a winner? When was the last time you saw yourself getting ahead of the game and succeeding in life? What is really holding you back? What are you really afraid of? Why won't you stop making excuses? Do you feel that your soul is empty? Are you searching for meaning? You need to ask yourself these questions before moving forward with your life. Once you can answer these questions honestly, you can began self-improvement and start your journey.

Your first step in your journey is accepting who you are and being okay with that. Understand that God made you the way you are and not everyone is meant to be 6'5 and athletic. Not everyone can score a 1600 on the SAT and get a full scholarship to an Ivy League School. Not everyone has the body of a swimsuit model or supermodel. Not everyone is going to be an executive of a Fortune 500 Company. Sometimes, we need to stop looking at our neighbor's lives and wishing that they were our own and start living the life that was intended for us. Accept who you are and decide from that moment on you want to change components in your life to be better and not settle for the status quo.

Once you realize that you want more out of life, you will not settle for ordinary but command the extraordinary. Often times, we go through life guessing with no clear direction. Now is the time that you develop your road map to success;

you are going to create a crystal clear strategy for your life. It's not how you start the game that's important but how you finish. So start playing the game of life today and enjoy it how it was meant for you to live.

While I was at an Anthony Robbins seminar (a renowned speaker), he said something so profound that I had to write it down because it was so relevant: "One reason so few of us achieve what we truly want is that we never direct our focus; we never concentrate our power. Most people dabble their way through life, never deciding to master anything in particular." When developing your strategy, you need laser focus!

What is your focus? Is your focus losing weight, making money, finding a meaning relationship, or job related? For example, if you want a promotion on your job, you need to know what job you are going after. You need to obtain additional knowledge. You may need to increase your education. You need to show that you are qualified. You need to become the expert for that position. You need to show that no one can be better than you for that particular job! By putting all of your effort and laser focus on one particular task, the results will come; you have to believe that when preparation meets opportunity there would be success.

Even if you don't find success right away when developing your strategy, don't become discouraged because it is only a stepping stone to success. Too often, we give up when one door closes and the opportunity seems glum.

When one opportunity door closes and all other opportunity doors appear to be sealed up tight, it's time to break an opportunity window and jump through. Winners find opportunities where others only see obstacles. Ineffectual weaklings sit around waiting for magical opportunity doors to open for them. Winners work for what they want and make it happen. Weaklings wait for what they want and hope it happens.
-Duane Alan Hahn

A quick tip that I have for you to jump-start your strategies is to have deadlines for today, this week, this month, 90 days' time, 6 months' time, and even 12 months' time. Deadlines written down create internal pressure that, when applied to your life, gives birth to creativity and activity whilst assisting your focus. This is a time management tool to focus your energy and behavior toward success.

When developing your map to success, I want you to visualize what you want your life to be like. What is your dream job? What is your ideal relationship? What kind of car do you see yourself driving? Do you want to own your own business? Do you want to travel across the country or out of the country this year or every year? This is your chance to have a massive brainstorming session in your head without reservation.

Your next step after visualization is to put it down on paper. Write down all your thoughts and ideas so you won't forget them. Then, rearrange them to put them in some form of chronological order so you have a timeline. This is an important step because soon you will attach goals to your thoughts and ideas. Writing it down on paper is the first step in bringing your thoughts to reality. A thought does not become reality until you put it on paper and take some form of action.

While you are writing down your thoughts and ideas of what you want for your life, I encourage you to think of people who could help you achieve success. Often times, it is impossible for people to accomplish success all on their own; they have a support system. Choose your support system wisely. There will be people who don't want to see you succeed because they are stuck in life's hardships. Only those who genuinely want your best interest should be your support system. Being around positive people generates more positive vibes from other people and yourself.

The next step in developing your strategy is to develop your goals; you must believe that it is at least possible for you to achieve your goal or you will not be motivated to try. More importantly, you must believe in your goals and yourself, even if others don't believe in you. However, just because you should believe that the goal is possible does not mean that you must expect it to be easy or even probable. What is important is that you are taking the necessary steps to change your life.

Taking action and following through is the next step. Think of a baseball pitcher as he stands at the mound. He first visualizes his pitch before he throws it, and then his goal is to throw a strike at the batter. There are many things going through his mind, but one thing for sure is his follow through. The pitcher needs to follow through with his arm when pitching the ball. The pitcher needs to follow through with getting three strikes and getting the batter out. The pitcher needs to follow through and get three batters out to be over with the inning. The pitcher also needs the support of his catcher to give him a good clue on what pitch to throw to be successful. He also needs the support of his pitching coach even before the game. A good pitcher has to be resilient, but his goals remain constant, and winning is the only option.

Developing your strategy for your life all begins with a thought, a thought of wanting the best life possible. Establishing goals and surrounding yourself with a supporting cast to assist you is vital. It's time for you to take your life back, get control over your own destiny, and start making things happen in your life. If you need to crawl first then crawl, then learn to walk, but soon you will be running; eventually, you will be flying with eagles. Don't limit yourself or tell yourself what you can't do. Focus on what you can accomplish and build on that.

Review

Six steps of Developing your Life Strategy

1. Visualize What You Want Out of Life
2. Write Your Goals Down and Organize
3. Choose Your Support System
4. Develop Your Goals
5. Implement Your Strategy
6. Live Your Best Life

Goals Tips

Interpersonal development and consciousness are lifelong pursuits because life is a work in progress. There will never be a day that will not require dedication, discipline, good judgment, energy, and the feeling that you can improve. Each day offers an opportunity for improvement. Each moment is an "advance or retreat" opportunity in the pursuit of your goals. Some of the best opportunities in life are the ones you create by the goals you set for your life. Every challenge you bring forth is one that you must conquer in order to move forward. Goals are nothing more than personal challenges that you set for personal development, professional development, and ultimately a better life. Here are some tips to consider when developing your goals:

- Dreams only turn into reality if you set a clear path to achieve them.
- Calculate how much time and effort it will take to achieve particular goals.

- Paint mental pictures to describe what your long-term future could look like.
- Evaluate any weaknesses or shortfalls in your capacity to meet your deadlines.
- Set goals that are specific, action-oriented, and realistic.
- Avoid setting goals that cannot be measured.
- Listen to any relevant directional feedback, both formal and informal.
- Find a mentor, someone who can help you toward achieving your goals.
- Ask people to share their goal successes to help motivate you.

Life is an ongoing journey with lots of beginnings and continuations. We never get to a point when all knowledge is attained and understood, when our bodies function flawlessly, when we completely honor our values, and achieve every goal.

Visualize what You want out of Life

Think back to when you were a child and had big dreams of what you wanted to be, maybe a ghost buster, firefighter, or a nurse. Maybe your dream was to own a home, be married with a dog, 2.5 kids, and the white picket fence. As you have gotten older, the dream has changed slightly, but you still want something more out of life. That dream has turned into something more because you are wiser and understand that you can actually have what you once thought was only a dream.

[40]

Believe that you are ENTITLED to have a family, house, career, car, wealth, health, or anything else you desire. If you put your trust in God, ask and He will give it to you. As long as you are doing your part, He will do his part and give you the desires of your heart because you are ENTITLED to it. I want you to list five things that you want for your life and implement them while you are developing your strategy.

1._____

2._____

3._____

4._____

5._____

We get better when we do better. And we do better when we know better. Personal development is the way that we purposely make everything count!

Strategies for Development

When you take steps on your path to greatness, there is no clear cut road on how to get there. Sometimes, you come to a crossroad and have to determine which way to go, which direction or path should your life be heading? This is your opportunity for a second chance at life to develop your road map to success the way God intended it to be. What talents could you play with? What is it that you do so well that you can design your life around it and be happy doing it? If you could look into the future and see yourself being everything you ever dreamed of, what would you see? Hold that vision. Here are some tips to ponder when developing your strategy:

- Be clear about what you want and don't want for your life.
- Be honest with yourself and your abilities.
- Identify your strengths and weaknesses.
- Build on what you know.
- Set boundaries to protect yourself from outside distractions.
- Be resilient in going after what you want.

You are responsible for your own personal development. It's a solo act. It is introspective thought and behavior modification. Self-improvement begins at home, inside our minds. Spend your life learning how to live. Living is a performance that requires you to work hard. If you're going to do it, do it well.

Bringing It Home

1. Be able to anticipate problems.
As long as you are living on this earth, you will encounter problems, but it is how you overcome your problems that matters the most. No one ever said that the road of life would be easy, and it's not. But you have to have faith that it will get better. By anticipating problems, sometimes the issues at hand don't seem as bad because you were prepared. For example, if you were driving and got a flat tire, you wouldn't feel as frustrated if you had a spare tire in the truck or AAA Road Service. The problem would not feel as bad because you anticipated there would eventually be a problem. Start thinking ahead of the game and looking down the road for potential problems. Be proactive instead of reactive.

2. Understand what you want out of life.
Any effort must begin with a sense of goals. What are your long-term goals and short-term goals? These goals need to be defined from the beginning and in a way that they can launch your future and be sustained over time. Goals serve as the foundation for planning. They tell you why there is a need to plan. Planning involves determining the actions to be taken to achieve particular goals. Some people say your goals should be compatible, practical, and attainable. But don't be afraid to reach for the stars because your potential is unlimited. What do you see for yourself in your thought life?

3. Time to grow and move.

Who are the people or influences in your life that you need to move out? This includes those who you have an informal, formal, or distant relationship with. If they are a support, keep them close and hold them dear. If there is a cancer in your life, it is vital to your success that it be removed, but Cancer is a disease that spreads like wild fire, and if not treated, it becomes fatal. As you grow and mature through life, you have to treat the cancer cells that try to hold you back from your destiny. Once you cure yourself from those people or situations, you are now free to move forward.

Thoughts

It's important not to focus on the goal so much that you lose sight of the underlying reason you set the goal in the first place. The world changes and so must you. While follow-through and persistence are among the most important traits related to long-term accomplishment, so is the ability to re-assess along the way. As long as you are honest with yourself, it is okay to change your mind, change goals mid-stream, shelve one for a later day, or cancel one altogether. Again, the trick is to be honest with yourself and not change your mind so frequently that you never accomplish anything.

Setbacks and failures are stepping stones to greatness. That statement is so profound I must repeat it again. Setbacks and failures are stepping stones to greatness. I have no doubt that you will encounter setbacks and failures on your journey, but you must have the dexterity and fortitude to withstand them and step on them on your way to greatness.

Get-It-Together

There is no time like the present to start making a change. The longer you wait, the longer it's going to take to get the results you want for your life. Over the next several days, you are going to start to develop your strategies for life. You will start the six step process with visualizing, and within the next 48 hours, you will write down your goals and organize your thoughts. It's time to start moving and flexing that mental muscle. Your destiny is waiting on you.

Faith

Faith is knowledge within the heart, beyond the reach of evidence

"Faith is accepting that you may not understand everything, but knowing that God will direct you to what He wants for your life."

~ Anonymous

"When you think your faith has failed you, all your hopes and dreams are gone, listen for the angel voice that whispers, "just hold on".

~ Anonymous

Where does faith come from? Are you born with it? Is it innate? Why is some people's faith stronger than others? Is faith something you can learn, and can you strengthen it? We will explore all of these questions.

Matthew 17:20: He replied, "Because you have so little faith. I tell you the truth, if you have faith as small as a mustard seed, you can say to this mountain, 'Move from here to there and it will move. Nothing will be impossible for you." In the physical I know you cannot move a mountain but in your life there are mountains/problems that seem to be insurmountable to move.

Nicole worked at a company for seven years as a HR Generalist and has been a loyal and faithful employee with desires to move up in the company. On that fateful Monday her manager came to her and said that they were restructuring the department, and her position was being eliminated. Nicole was devastated by the news and wondered how this could happen when she gave 110% every day for seven years.

Nicole decided that she was not going to wallow in self-pity by the decisions of one person but take this as an opportunity for growth in her career. She spent seven years in the same position without any opportunity for growth. She updated her resume and sent it out and within 30 days she had another offer from a pharmaceutical company. Nicole did not allow doubt to set in; she did not worry about where her next paycheck would come from once unemployed. She took her setback and made it into a comeback because her faith was so strong that she knew that she would not become unemployed.

Faith is defined as confidence or trust in a person, thing, deity, in the doctrines or teachings of a religion, or view. It can also be belief that is not based on proof. In life, you need to believe even when the evidence, proof or success is not readily in front of you. You need to believe that the outcome will happen in your favor.

In 2007 Debra's mother died from triple negative breast cancer. Diagnosed when she was 61, she fought a good fight for 4 years. Debra stood by her side through every doctor's appointment and every treatment. The night Debra's mother died Debra held her hand and watched as her mother took her last breath. Debra misses her mother every day, especially because on March 7th, after having a mammogram, Debra was told that she had the same breast cancer that took her mom from her.

She remembered walking into the doctor's office to get her results. A doctor and a nurse brought her into a room and asked that she be seated. The next words she heard were, "Debra I'm sorry to inform you that you have breast cancer." Basically in shock, she didn't hear much after that. Her mind couldn't grasp the fact that she now had cancer.

After a biopsy confirmed the worst, Debra was scheduled for surgery. She chose a bilateral mastectomy because of her history. It wasn't until they sent the cancerous tissue off, she found out it was triple negative, a very aggressive breast cancer. After the surgery Debra began chemo, and like her mother she refused to let cancer rule her life.

Debra stated, "This is not my death sentence but a challenge that has made me stronger and will continue to do so. My faith sustains me and my full recovery is just around the corner." Even in the mist of Debra's storm she moved mountains, with her faith, to beat cancer. She did not allow the disease to overtake her life; she kept a positive attitude and believed that she would live and be cured.

James 1:3 says "...because you know that the testing of your faith develops perseverance." The definition of perseverance is steadfastness in doing something despite difficulty or delay in achieving success. So when developing your perseverance you are strengthening your faith. Your faith is now steadfast and you have to believe that in the midst of any storm, any problem, or any difficulty that success will still arise.

Faith is something you can learn and strengthen; it is the will of the mind and heart. You have to learn how to believe in yourself and in a higher power. Like any muscle in the human body, in order to build and strengthen that muscle you have to exercise it on a regular basis. Strengthening your faith is no different. You have to make up your mind to believe. No matter how many times you may fail at something you have to believe that you will succeed at some point. 2 Timothy 4:7 says, "I have fought the good fight, I have finished the race, I have kept the faith."

Gandhi's Views On Faith

Mahatma Gandhi was deeply interested in the comparative study of religions since the days of his youth. Gandhi's life, ideas and work are of crucial importance to all those who want a better life for humankind. His mission was not only to humanize religion, but also to moralize it. Gandhi's interpretation of Hinduism, Islam, and Christianity made his religion a federation of different religious faiths. Below are three excerpts from the *"Mind of Mahatma Gandhi."* See how he interprets faith.

- It is faith that steers us through stormy seas, faith that moves mountains and faith that jumps across the ocean. That faith is nothing but a living, wide-awake consciousness of God within. He who has achieved that faith wants nothing. Bodily diseased, he is spiritually healthy; physically poor, he rolls in spiritual riches. (YI, 24-9-1925, p. 331)
- Without faith this world would come to naught in a moment. True faith is appropriation of the reasoned experience

of people whom we believe to have lived a life purified by prayer and penance. Belief, therefore, in prophets or incarnations who have lived in remote ages is not an idle superstition but a satisfaction of an inmost spiritual want. (YI, 14-4-1927, p. 120)

- Faith is not a delicate flower, which would wither under the slightest stormy weather. Faith is like the Himalaya Mountains which cannot possibly change. No storm can possibly remove the Himalaya Mountains from their foundations. ... And I want every one of you to cultivate that faith in God and religion. (H, 26-1-1934, p. 8)

Gandhi was a prophetic thinker who spent countless years of his life on the causes he believed in due to his faith in God. Gandhi provided the world some of the best quotes that made us think and reflect. It is now your time to think and reflect on some of Gandhi's quotes. When you read these quotes what is your interpretation, what does it mean to you?

My faith is brightest in the midst of impenetrable darkness.

_____
_____
_____
_____
_____
_____

Every living faith must have within itself the power of rejuvenation if it is to live.

_____
_____
_____
_____
_____
_____

What is faith worth if it is not translated into action?

_____
_____
_____
_____
_____

A living faith cannot be manufactured by the rule of majority.

_____
_____
_____
_____
_____

Faith is gained in strength only when people are willing to lay down their lives for it.

_____
_____
_____
_____

Bringing It Home

1. **Learn from failure.**
   Instead of viewing your failures as failures, view them as learning opportunities. Don't let your failures shake your faith into believing that you will not succeed. Everything that goes wrong in your life is an opportunity to learn, so embrace it.

2. **Try, even when you feel like you can't or shouldn't.**
   Sometimes we feel like we shouldn't do something new because we might do it wrong. This is a bad mindset. Instead, give yourself permission to try something, even if you might get it wrong. If you never try new things, you'll never be able to make progress. Develop a mindset of faith.

3. **Focus on moving forward.**
   Stop getting stuck in the past and focusing on when you "used to be good" or the mistakes you made back then. No matter if you think you were better then or worse, the only thing you should worry about is doing well in the future. You can't change the past but you can have a better future, so put all of your energy into that instead of worrying about what you can't change. Let your faith be the guiding force to moving forward in your life.

4. Love yourself for who you are.

Don't try to be someone you're not or be upset with yourself for the things that you think are wrong with you. Faith is nothing more than believing in yourself, and that you can and will accomplish a goal, task or feat. Love yourself regardless of the outcome because you are worth it.

Thoughts

Faith, from my point of view, can mean belief in things hoped for, the trust in things you have not seen but believe in its reality. Faith means having so much trust in what you want that you don't need any explanation or justification from anywhere. You won't need to doubt what you want, want you can't see or investigate the problem because you have faith for manifestation. Some faith is exercised toward God or a higher power they believe in. At the end of the day you need to have faith in something and yourself.

Get-It-Together

2 Corinthians 5:7 says, "We live by faith, not by sight." Just because you cannot always see the outcome does not mean that the outcome will not end in your favor. I challenge you to write down things that you want in life; it may be a new job, restored health, a child, or someone to love. Whatever you write down, I want you to post it on your wall where you can see it every

day so it is a constant reminder that it is the desire of your heart. Now that you have written it down now is the time to take action to get what you desire. Remember James 2:26 "Faith without work is dead."

Communication

Without it, Chaos Erupts

"The problem with communication ... is the illusion that it has been accomplished."

-George Bernard Shaw

"What we've got here is a failure to communicate."

Film buffs regard that line as one of the most memorable in movie history. It was spoken by the actor Strother Martin in the 1967 feature "Cool Hand Luke," starring Paul Newman. For those who haven't seen the film, it takes place in a Southern prison camp and centers on the title character's (Newman) refusal to submit to the camp's dehumanizing routine and the warden's (Martin) determination to break Luke's spirit and force him to conform.

Comedic actor Damon Wayans, in the 1995 feature film "Major Payne," spoke the same line. Wayans plays a near-maniacal Army Major assigned to whip a detail of dysfunctional children into shape to win a war games competition. Both movies dealt with communication and different means to achieve it.

Is it possible to live your best life or the life you always wanted to live without being able to communicate with other people? Before moving ahead, consider the following questions: How do you effectively communicate with those around you? Do you bring out the best or worst in people? Do you have the ability to successfully get your point across without being sarcastic? How do others view your communication skills?

We know that authentic communication is both verbal and nonverbal. It is not always what you say to people, it is how you treat them that matters also. I have always found that communication is not just in the words that we speak; it's also how we say it. I believe communication comes first from a thought in the brain, and then processes to what that person wants to convey whether it be positive or negative. It is a conscious thought that is processed before you take any action in your life.

How you communicate your thoughts and ideas is at the heart of your personal and professional success. Good communicators obtain results and encourage open and co-operative communication from others. The first step in good communication is communicating positively and adopting a positive attitude. Believe it or not, positivity breeds more positivity, and you welcome that kind of energy. Anything less is unacceptable.

In my travels, the most important limitations on people's perceptions are often based on cultural and emotional differences. Most of us, generally speaking, perceive what we expect to perceive. In other words, we see what we expect to see and, to a very large extent, hear what we want to hear. We tend to communicate with others and think our message is being conveyed effectively. However, what often happens is that the message has not actually been received at all because of miscommunication. It has been neither seen nor heard. It has been ignored.

When this happens, effective communication breaks down.

So, before we communicate effectively, we must consider whether or not we understand what the recipient expects to see or hear. Not an easy task. If you are able to do this, you can then make reasonable assumptions about what their expectations are.

When we communicate, there are always demands. Communication demands that the recipient becomes involved and receives something. If the communication gels with the aspirations, the values, and the point of view of the recipient, it is a powerful thing. However, if it goes against the goals and ambitions of that particular individual, it is highly likely that the communication will either not be received at all or meet stiff resistance.

Contrary to what some people might say, the solution to effective communication is simplicity. Don't try to over-analyze the situation if you want to connect with people. Just keep it simple; be clear and concise. In your thought life, it is easy to misjudge, misconstrue, or misinterpret information given to you or what someone might be sharing with you. Take time to consider the other person's point of view, as there are many sides of a story that are not yours.

We have all seen people who think they are effective communicators but are far from it. Debbie F., who is employed as a school teacher, believes she is the most effective communicator, both verbally and in writing. However, there are aspects of her communication style that don't mesh well with others. When you try to coach her or provide her with feedback on her communication style or aspects of her performance, rather than taking the feedback as information to help her improve, she views it as criticism and acts out poorly because she does not know how to accept developmental feedback. Because she is unaware that she "receives" information in a completely different way than how it was intended, she will remain "stuck" in many aspects of her personal and professional life.

What Debbie does not realize is that her lack of not wanting to change not only affects her but every student in her class that she comes in contact with. Accepting help and constructive criticism can help her become a better educator and person. Don't be like Debbie and be in the "stuck zone" of always wanting to be right and not wanting to see your faults.

Can you truly reach your fullest potential in life without having effective and authentic communication? The answer to that question is simply no! At some point in life, the pure interaction you have with others will determine how far you will get in business, relationships, and family; communication is in everything that we do. Be prepared to examine and identify your strengths and weaknesses as a communicator.

You also need to determine if you are better at verbal or nonverbal communication? If you know that you are better at listening, then use that strength to communicate with others. However, if you are not good at listening, then you need to restate what you are hearing from the other person so that you can get clarity for yourself. If you have the gift of gap, then use it! However, be careful with that gift because you can talk so much that you lose your audience. When talking, always make sure the other people understand what you are saying and not just nodding their heads like a bobble head.

What is your body language saying? Believe it or not, you can have an entire conversation without saying a word. Did you know you could turn someone off merely because of your body language? Is your body language saying that you are unapproachable by folding your arms and frowning? If so, you are telling people that you don't want to be bothered and are not interested. During conversations, do you make eye contact with the person you are talking to? I am not saying give someone the evil eye but make good eye contact to let the person know that you are engaged?

Women, how many times have you had a conversation while playing with your hair? Twisting, pulling, curling, or flipping your hair is a total distraction during a conversation or in a meeting. A lot of the time it is not what you say that makes the difference; it is what you do! A colleague of mine told me that he was interviewing a highly qualified candidate from Harvard University for an Assistant Professor position in English. Although her qualifications were stellar, he could not get past her flipping and twisting her hair throughout the entire interview. He commented how it was distracting; ultimately, she did not get the job.

Doing it Right

There are good ways to communicate and not-so-good ways to communicate; you have to decide which method is most effective to get your point across, how people may receive you, and how you will be remembered. An important lesson in communicating with others is recognizing your strengths and weaknesses.

Steps to take to become a better communicator:

- Listen to what people tell you and give them your full attention.
- Be approachable.
- Don't make assumptions about the other person's motives, attitudes, character, etc.
- Be sure to communicate to the right person.
- Be sure to communicate the real issues.
- Observe and be willing to verify the information you receive.
- Ask questions. Don't assume you understand what a person means.
- Don't take everything personally.

Developing credibility is probably the most important element of communication and is reflected in the degree to which people trust what you say. Communicating with a positive approach is presented as an essential skill. Ideas are suggested for practicing the positive approach and for being realistic about expectations of individuals. Providing feedback that is high in information is an important skill. Credible people praise good behavior and tell you what is good about it. They also give specific instructions for improvement.

Communicating with consistency, learning how to listen, and improving nonverbal communication are proposed as essential communication skills. Consistently communicated messages build credibility and trust. One can learn good listening skills by concentrating on listening, not interrupting, and respecting a person's right to express views.

Communication is the Key

Your success or failure to communicate effectively will shape and perhaps determine whether or not you achieve your personal or professional goals. It will affect your self-esteem, sense of well-being, and contributions you make to your family, your job, and your community. Good or bad communication can even affect your health. The way you communicate is tied to how you perceive a situation or an issue at that point as well as your reaction to it. How well do you communicate with others? Below are several questions to find out just how well you communicate with other people. Normally, there would be a formal rating assessed with these questions. But, I want you to look at them and give yourself an honest self-assessment.

Rate yourself from 1 to 5
1= almost always; 2 = very frequently;
3 = frequently; 4 = occasionally; 5 = almost never

Rating

1. I look at the feelings or emotions behind the words people are using. __
2. I maintain good eye contact and give people my full attention. __
3. I carefully probe when I do not fully understand something. __
4. I use open ended questions to get people to explain their ideas. __
5. I do not interrupt when other people are talking. __
6. People who know me would say that I am a good listener. __
7. I quickly notice changes in tone or intonation. __
8. I am good at reading "between the lines" when necessary. __
9. I focus on the facts in giving and receiving feedback. __
10. I change my communication style according to the situation. __

Once you have rated yourself, look at your strengths in communicating and then look at your weakness. The areas with the highest ratings are the ones you will need to focus on and be committed to strengthening. Ask yourself the question, "What can I do to become a better communicator and how will it impact my life?"

Five Steps to Better Communication

Effective communication becomes even more crucial during high-stress times, like holidays. Little things can seem much bigger on important days that come with high expectations. Make a conscious effort to practice the following basic communication skills:

- **Listening** - *Effective listening requires concentration, tolerance, and sensitivity. Concentration means focusing solely on what the speaker is saying.*

- **Expressing Yourself** – *First, you need to listen to yourself to know what you want to get across. If you feel confused, spend a few quiet moments going over your thoughts. Then, you'll be ready to state your message clearly.*

- **Interpreting Body Language** - *It's difficult to explain nonverbal communication in words. Yet, it is a vital form of communication. It is possible to understand how the other person is receiving your* *message through clues in his or her movements.*

- **Being aware of your differences** – *Someone's perception of the same event or piece of information can vary a great deal. Different backgrounds lead to different expectations, and we tend to hear what we expect to hear.*

- **Resolving Conflict** - *Conflicts can occur for many reasons, including "black and white thinking," clashing standards or beliefs, unresolved childhood issues, and the background stress of modern life. Conflicts potentially can be useful and channeled in healthy ways as long as they don't involve threats or stubbornness.*

Bringing It Home

1. Never confuse talking and communicating
A little self-examination about what you say and how you say it can mean the difference between a listener tuning you out and hanging on to your every word. You want people to respect you, your advice, your thoughts, and your feelings. Never try to over-talk someone because you are trying to make a point. Ask the person if he/she understands what you are trying to convey and then ask for feedback. There is a distinct difference between talking to someone and talking at them.

2. Shut up and Listen

Most of us do not realize the importance of listening as a communicative tool. Yet, studies have shown that we actually spend 50% more time listening than we do talking. We often take listening for granted, never realizing that it is a skill that can be learned. This pearl of wisdom is particularly precious, "Say something when you have something to say. If you don't know what you're talking about, shut up." Very helpful!

3. How to get the most out of people

Credibility precedes great communication. People will follow you when they trust you and feel a sense of comfort. You need to be authentic in your actions and communication. Live by example. When you live your life a certain way, others will see that you are a person of great value. Your communication will speak volumes by your actions rather than your words.

Thoughts

Before you open your mouth, it helps to think about what it is that you want to achieve by initiating the conversation - the message you send should be aimed at starting some sort of appropriate action, to change or influence someone's way of thinking or mindset. It is important to be clear in your mind what your most important objective or goal is. Then, choose an appropriate language style or tone that helps to achieve your goal. The more focused you are in your message, the greater the possibility of its success.

Get-It-Together

Striving to be better on a daily basis should be one of your goals. In this day and age, it is a hard goal to accomplish when there are many negative people and influences out there. I challenge you to get out of your comfort zone and start communicating with people that you would not normally work, socialize, or mingle with. Think outside the box and expand your horizons. This will allow you to grow and increase your communication skills. If you are able to adapt to your new environment, your old environment will be a piece of cake. Remember, sometimes all it takes is a warm smile to start a conversation.

Relationships

Being True to Yourself first, then Allowing Others in

"Few things help an individual more than to place responsibility upon him, and to let him know that you trust him."
-Booker T. Washington

How many times have you entered into a relationship and it was not what you thought it would be? In the beginning, the relationship had so much potential and the possibilities seemed endless. You spent so much time with this person and got accustomed to them being there. You thought that they were "The One." Sometimes, it seems like an endless cycle of meeting the wrong person.

Have you ever questioned yourself as to why you keep meeting the wrong person? How come you can't meet the person God has for you? If you looked at your past relationships, I am willing to bet that there is a consistency with your ex's. Sometimes, we are drawn to the same type of people because we are attracted to them. However, the downside is you will continue to have the same problems because you are dating the same type of person. The flip side to this is that if you dated ten people and found something wrong with all of them, maybe the problem was not them; the problem could be you.

Never lose yourself in a relationship! In every positive relationship, the fundamental goal is to be happy; however, too often, instead of pursuing your goals, you start making your dreams and goals secondary. Then, you constantly ask yourself the questions, "Where did I go wrong. How could I not see that this person was not the right person for me? Was I that much in love? Was I blinded from the truth?"

In life, we all fantasize about marriage, kids, and our future without ever really asking the tough questions: What truly makes me happy? What am I willing to sacrifice in a relationship? Can I not be selfish and compromise? What is my definition of a life partner? In relationships, our imagination gets us into trouble at times because we tend to choose people who we think we want instead of choosing people we need in our lives. Sadly, these types of relationships lead to heartache, unhealthy relationships, bad marriages, and divorce.

Well, did you ever think that maybe it was not you? That it could just be the other person who did not appreciate you and that they were selfish? The problem is that early on in the relationship you were given signs that you chose to neglect. I call these signs *The Writing on the Wall.* I believe God sends us warning signs that we are headed for trouble or signs that we are going in the wrong direction, but we choose to ignore God's signs. You may be going through a situation and ask God for guidance, but because His guidance does not come in the form that you want, you totally ignore what He is telling you. It is your job to recognize those signs!

Some people call it having a sixth sense, woman's intuition, a bad feeling, a gut feeling, or God speaking to them. Whatever you want to call it does not matter; just believe that it is real, and you should acknowledge those feelings. Sometimes, *The Writing on the Wall* is crystal clear; other times, it is extremely vague. You have to determine what is right? What is real? What is honest? What is genuine? Do you lead with your heart or do you lead with your head?

It is important to be in tune with yourself in order to recognize *The Writing on the Wall*. For example, if you are dating a person with children and want to pursue a long-term relationship, ask yourself how the person interacts with his or her own children or around your friends. If that male or female constantly uses profanity in front of their his or her children or friends, what makes you think that he or she won't do the same thing if you have a child together? This is a sign, and if you ignore it and conceive a child with this person, the same fate is waiting for you and your expected child.

In life, we tend to make excuses. We think over a period of time that people will change, or we think that we can change them. Realistically, we know that not to be true, but that does not stop people from trying. The divorce rate in America is representative of marriages ending because the person ended up not being who you thought they were.

Loving someone or being in love with someone is a hard thing to do in this day and age. It's hard because it takes so much work and commitment; many times, the hard work and commitment are only coming from one person. Sometimes, when in love, we lose our self-worth, self-value, or just lose ourselves. We focus so much on the fact of being in love that we don't see, or chose not to see, *The Writing on the Wall.*

Many times, when things are not going well in your relationships, your heightened sense of reasoning has diminished so you tolerate behavior that is unacceptable. Your thought patterns are not clear; therefore, you continually make excuses for that person because you are in love. Are you really in love? Or are you in love with the thought or idea of what being in love is supposed to be? You start asking yourself thought provoking questions like how you got yourself into this situation. Where did all the time go? Then, you wake up one morning and wonder who this person is that you are sleeping next to.

I believe we put ourselves in situations, and sometimes, we neglect the obvious. We often sell ourselves short and settle for second best. But do you think that God put you on this earth to have second best? Why should you settle for second best? If you love yourself first, then demand that your partner loves you the same way. You should always have genuine love.

Don't Lose Yourself

There is only one *you* who have been uniquely created, so you have to take care of you first, no matter what. Too many times, people put others' needs in front of their own and neglect themselves to the point of destruction. If you are not able to function, how are you able to take care of yourself or anyone else? Consider the following statements to gauge whether or not you are losing yourself in your relationships:

- ❑ I put up with rude or inappropriate comments or behaviors.
- ❑ I am too busy to treat myself to anything special.
- ❑ I am uncomfortable saying no when I don't want to do something.
- ❑ I consistently put everyone's needs and wants before my own.
- ❑ I don't feel that I am worth a lot of attention.
- ❑ If I am not feeling well, I perform anyway to please my partner.
- ❑ I feel my opinion does not matter as much to my partner as other people's opinions.
- ❑ It's hard for me to walk away because I am nothing without them.

If you check any of these boxes, you have some soul searching to do. Somehow, you have lost yourself in the midst of your relationship. It's okay because it's not too late to recover and get back your true self.

Building Trust

Trust doesn't just naturally happen between two people, even if they think they love each other unconditionally. It takes hard work; if you've been hurt in the past, it can be especially difficult. Building trust takes time; you need to prove to your partner that you are trustworthy and that you trust them in return. If your partner has trouble trusting, you can do a lot to create an environment where trust can be nurtured. Listen to your partner, respect them and their opinions, and accept them as they are. Reveal parts of your own past, show them that you trust them, and you will help them to do the same. If you are vulnerable, it helps your partner feel that he/she is safe to be vulnerable as well.

Don't rush it. If you truly love your partner and want what's best for them, you'll wait. If you're in a relationship with someone you feel you can't trust, don't ignore it. If you have trouble trusting anyone, you might want to seek counseling before you run away from what could be a good relationship. Your past does affect your ability to trust. However, if trust hasn't been a problem for you in the past and your gut is telling you to protect yourself from this person, take it as a sign. Take a close look at who they are, how they treat others, and how they treat you. Your gut may be giving you good information. Remember *The Writing on the Wall* is always there.

Bringing It Home

1. The Ability to Understand
An important part of building a happy life is
creating a balance among work, personal, and
family needs that allows you to pursue your
dreams, achieve your goals, and enhance your
physical and emotional well-being. If we first
took the time and established a clear
understanding of our situation, we would be
better off. In a relationship, make sure that your
partner understands you and that you
understand your partner. In addition, the level
of understanding between you and your partner
should be apparent. Stop thinking like you used
to and see the world not as it is but as we are.

2. Communicating with Your Partner
Most people agree that the ability to effectively
communicate with others can have a huge
impact on interpersonal relationships. Learning
how to say what you mean in a way that others
will understand can eliminate many stresses on
relationships.

1. **Be Aware of Non-Verbal Signals.** Our body
   language - facial expressions, posture, eye
   contact - all change the meaning given to our
   words. Our voice expressions - tone, volume,
   rhythm - all show the feeling in our words.
   Work to match your non-verbal
   communication with what you are saying so
   that your message carries the meaning that
   you want.

2. **Listen.** Indicate that you are paying attention
   by nodding your head or using brief

statements. Do not interrupt when you are listening. Let the speaker finish speaking before you jump in. Keep an open mind and be non-judgmental.

3. **Paraphrase and Ask Questions.** Repeat back what you think you've heard someone say and use summary statements. Ask questions to clarify statements. These techniques help you to avoid misunderstandings.

3. Love Yourself then Love Someone Else
Self-love means that your love comes from within and is generated from within, not from "loving" any object because it may please you tremendously, whether that object is someone else or yourself. The art of loving yourself begins with self-acceptance. You begin loving yourself when you stop rejecting yourself, especially on the feeling level.

Now that you love yourself wholeheartedly, go and love someone else. Feel free to explore and love without guilt, anger, or bitterness.

Thoughts

Many people will come into your life, and you have to decide whether or not to let those people into your inner circle. Your inner circle should be intimate, sacred, and trusting. You should be at peace with those people in your inner circle and comforted to know that they support you at all cost.

How do you know whom you should let into your inner circle? Well, those people are the ones who hurt when you hurt, cry when you cry, and laugh when you laugh. Sometimes, they are the voice of reason when things are not clear in your head. Your inner circle goes beyond your immediate family; they are the ones who support you in your time of need and cheer you on in your victories.

In our society, we have developed a special compulsiveness about one specific kind of relationship: romantic love. We search for a partner; we hunger for intimate relationship, but satisfaction often remains elusive. Your Thought Life may sometimes make you feel like you can't go on because you feel hurt, destroyed, or neglected. Your weeping is only temporary. Sometimes, God takes something away from you to prepare you for something greater.

Get-It-Together

God made Adam and was happy with His creation but saw that he was lonely, so He created Eve for Adam's companionship. God wants men and women to have a happy union and be blissful in that relationship. If you are in a relationship, I challenge you to take a good look at your relationship. Are you really happy? If not, what can you do to make it better? Ask yourself, "Am I in the relationship that God has intended for me?" Look at every situation and look at yourself in the process; it might be time for healing, forgiving, or loving. Don't let the devil keep you from the person that God has for you.

Fear

What We don't Know Frightens Us

Never say never, because limits, like fears, are often just an illusion.

-Michael Jordon

Only when we are no longer afraid do we begin to live.

-Dorothy Thompson

Did you know the meaning of fear when you were a young child? Probably not, at least until someone that you trusted or looked up to told you what it was. Mankind has simply connected a word to a feeling, giving it life and in turn making people fear it. Fear is not something God gives us, "For God hath not given us the spirit of fear; but of power, and of love, and of a sound mind" (2 Timothy 1:7).

Are we born with fear or is it something taught? Some infants will crawl right off the side of a bed without hesitation and without fear because they don't know any better. Other toddlers will go near a hot stove and try to touch it. Through experience, children learn what they can and cannot do. This does not mean they fear things; they simply are increasing their knowledge. However, as adults, we have a number of fears such as fear of heights, so we won't go on airplanes, on top of roofs or up stepladders because of fear. Is fear taught? Or are we really born with fear? For many people, fear is simply a thought; it is an image ingrained in our minds.

You probably have dreams, hopes, and aspirations for your life. There are things you'd like to do and try. Maybe you imagine writing, teaching, moving into another specialty, or applying for an interesting position at work. Maybe you've even contemplated moving up the management ladder or taking on some added responsibilities.

For one reason or another, many people never follow their dreams and never do many of the things they want to do in life or venture far from where they are right now. Often, our fears hold us back. We don't want to look foolish, be embarrassed, or feel like a novice. We fear failure, fear success, and fear the unknown.

Would you believe that confident, successful people are afraid of making changes, trying new things, and venturing into uncharted waters with their career? But they've somehow managed to move forward in spite of their fears. If successful people have fears and are able to move forward, reflect on your life. How can you work through your fears and toward greater happiness and success? What you have to do is change your thought pattern; if you think you're going to fail, then most likely you will fail. If you think or feel afraid, then you are going to be afraid. Let that fear or feeling go, and just do it. If you fall, get back up.

Fear is a basic emotional sensation and response system initiated by an aversion to some perceived risk or threat. Fear also can be described as a feeling of extreme dislike toward certain conditions, objects, people, or situations such as: fear of darkness, fear of ghosts, etc. Personal fear varies extremely in degree from mild caution to extreme phobia and paranoia.

Fear will consume your conscious life, spiritual life, and actual life. Your thought life will cease to exist because you will not allow yourself to grow because of thoughts of inadequacy, thoughts of depression, thoughts of inequality, thoughts of tribulation. etc. As long as you focus on the problem and not the solution, you will always stay stuck in your thought life and never move to your purpose in life and fulfill your destiny. A great quote to remember when facing fear is "Only when we are no longer afraid do we begin to live." - Dorothy Thompson

Know that every time you stretch yourself in some way or try something new, fear will automatically be a part of the equation. Rather than looking at it as a bad thing, acknowledge that you are stepping out of your comfort zone. Think of it more as "growing pains." If you didn't feel that fear, you wouldn't be challenging yourself. Once you master a new skill or gain some experience, the fear will start to dissipate — until your next challenge!

Fear is a very important factor in intractable conflict. Emotions like fear can often cause extreme and seemingly irrational behavior in people, which can result in escalating conflict. It is not the only motivating factor behind political violence, or necessarily the most obvious, but it is virtually always there. Whenever I ask why people hate or why they are willing to kill or die for a cause, the answer is invariably linked to fear.

Fear is a natural reaction to the challenges of life, but in order to follow your steps to success, you must confront yours fears. Remember that famous quote by Franklin Roosevelt, "The only thing we have to fear is fear itself." When you hear that, what does it mean to you? You must learn how to confront and defeat your fears, instead of allowing them to take a hold of you. If you don't, you will never experience the life you were meant to live.

Fear is nothing more than an emotion that you can learn to control. Think back to when you were a child learning to ride a bike; you didn't want your training wheels off or you didn't want your parents to let go of you because you had a fear of falling. When the training wheels came off and you started to ride by yourself, you might have fallen once or twice, but after you fell, the fear was gone. You gained confidence to get back up, dust yourself off, and ride again. Apply the same principle to your life right now. Why not get out there and start a new business, lose 50lbs, get into another relationship, go after that promotion, or attempt to have another baby; whatever it might be that you are letting fear hold you back from doing, simply go out and do.

What is it in life that is so big, so grand, so enormous that you could lose that you are fearful of? Anything that is worth having is worth fighting for, so there should be nothing out there that should keep you from your destiny?

Identifying Fear

Fear is a painful emotion or passion excited by the expectation of evil, or the apprehension of impending danger; apprehension; anxiety; solicitude; or alarm. List four areas in your life that you feel fear is holding you back:

1._____

2._____

3._____

4._____

It is important to acknowledge those areas that are keeping you bound and tied down. Until you are able to overcome these fears, you will not be able to go any further with your life and fulfill your destiny. You have greatness in you; don't let fear consume you. It's time to overcome whatever has been holding you back.

Overcoming Fear

Fear comes from more of the unknown; you have to increase your knowledge to overcome it. Fear is simply a state of mind. You cannot allow a person or situation to hold you captive and keep you from your destiny. The more creative you are, the more you can explore new ideas to release your inner strength and come out of your situation. To overcome fear, you have to know what it sounds like. Often times, it will sound like this:

- *I don't know if I am capable of pulling that off.*

- *You are the underdog. How are you going to compete with the big boys?*

- *If you fail, how are you going to recover? Did you ever think about that?*

- *You are going into uncharted waters. Do you have the stamina for this?*

- *You can't win!*

- *You're not smart enough; you don't have enough education, enough experience, enough money, enough talent...*

Well, tell all those people who said you could not do it or did not believe in your dream to "stick it." You will succeed, you will make it, you will be better, and you will be more powerful than ever.

Once you know what fear sounds like, you can avoid pitfalls, people, and situations. The more confidence you gain in yourself, the less you are fearful about your situation. Believe that God has given you a talent, and decide that you are going to use it fearlessly.

Bringing It Home

1. What Fear is holding you back?
What are the areas of your life where fear is
holding you back? Could it be your career; you
feel like you're stuck in a dead-end job, and your
life is not going anywhere. Or you're not getting
that promotion you wanted and fear you will
have to wait another year for it. Or are you
afraid to start that business venture you always
talked about. Maybe it's financial; you're up to
your armpits in debt and are barely making
ends meet; is your fear? Your relationship is in a
downward spiral, and your fear is that you are
not sure that you can recover. Whatever your
fear might be, it is important that you identify it
so that you can address the problem. I could
come up with a hundred different types of fears,
but the fears are not the problem. You not
conquering your fears are the problem.

2. Conquer your Fear
In order to conquer fear, you have to start by
accepting, addressing, and overcoming the
things that you fear the most. After doing so,
you will look back and think how foolish it was
to be afraid in the first place. Learn to leave your
comfort zone. When you leave your comfort zone,
you become a more versatile individual. People
fear the unknown, but if you venture out and
take the risk to conquer your fear, you will
eventually adapt to your situation. We will no
longer fear something once we attack it,
accomplish it, or achieve some form of success
over it. The next time similar situations arise,

you will no longer stress over it; instead, you will just do it.

3. Personal Fear
There are many ways of approaching fear in the context of conflict. However, since fear is such a personal issue, most approaches focus on the individual. Some ways to deal with your fear include:

- Becoming aware of it
- Identifying the ways you express fear
- Recognizing the situations which trigger fear
- Using behavioral techniques to reduce fear and stress

Once you understand and can change some of the beliefs that have been programmed into you by society, you can take control of your life. You can also determine your destiny through the power of positive thought. Become successful in any aspect of your life that you choose. You just have to get past one thing, yourself. You just need to walk through that door that has been opened for you all along.

4. Societal Fears
In order to overcome fears, individuals and groups must first come to terms with their fears and understand just how destructive they can be. However, it is equally important to be aware of others' fears. Being aware of other people's fear allows you to deal with it appropriately. One of the most effective ways of handling the fear of

others is through empathy, or seeing things from the other person's perspective.

Thoughts

We must set our minds on always conquering the unknown. Always "think outside the box." Look fear in the eyes and just do the task. Chances are that you will succeed and soon come to find out that fear is nothing more than a word. Every great person has undoubtedly faced fear many times, yet they have succeeded in their life. So can you! "Neither a man nor a crowd nor a nation can be trusted to act humanely or to think sanely under the influence of a great fear." - Bertrand Russell

When fear is the motivation for pursuing and attaining material goals, that fear is not eliminated by the attainment of those goals. On the contrary, when we acquire more, we think we need more, and the cycle never ends. Of course, we have legitimate needs that must be met, but what's important is our sense of discernment. Lack of integration means we will be unrealistic in determining what our real needs are and will never be satisfied, no matter how much we have.

As long as you're stretching yourself and moving forward with your life, some degree of fear will always be there reminding you that you're challenging yourself. Rather than making fear an obstacle, learn to work through it to accomplish your goals and make your dreams come true. One of my favorite motivational speakers, Les Brown, once said, "Fear death if you will, but never fear life." Is it scary to try new things, to expand your horizons? You bet, but it can also be exhilarating — and that's what life is all about.

Get-It-Together

You now know that Fear is a state of mind and a phobia. The toughest part is confronting your fear, but once you have accomplished that, you are well on your way to being fearless. Your challenge is conquering your fear wall. In this chapter, you listed four fears that made up your fear wall. In the next 48 hours, you will choose one of those fears and start the process of overcoming it. You will continue until you have eliminated all four fears and have torn down your fear wall.

Challenges/ Obstacles

Overcoming What's is in your Path

Then, without realizing it, you try to improve yourself at the start of each new day; of course, you achieve quite a lot in the course of time. Anyone can do this, it costs nothing and is certainly very helpful. Whoever doesn't know it must learn and find by experience that a quiet conscience makes one strong.

-Anne Frank

Life is created with many obstacles, hurdles, and challenges; in fact, problems do not discriminate. It does not matter whether you are white, black, brown, or red, when life comes at you hard, it comes fearlessly. Some people are born with a silver spoon in their mouth and extreme wealth, but that does not protect them from health problems, accidents, or bad relationships. That is just a part of life, and we just have to keep living and overcome what life throws our way. There is no clear cut method to avoid pitfalls, but here are some rules to live by when overcoming challenges.

First, nothing is impossible if you want it badly enough. You will make every sacrifice known to man to make your dream a reality. That means if you need to break your addiction to smoking, drinking, drugs, gambling, etc...you will take the necessary steps to make it happen. You might need to start losing weight to save your life. So start going to the gym, walk around the block, and start eating healthy.

You may have just been diagnosed with diabetes or high blood pressure and now your health is at risk. Being put on medication at the age of 30 is not what you had planned. It is vital for you to start eating a healthy diet, working out, and living a stress free life as much as possible. If you want it badly enough, you will make it happen, whether it's for your health or your financial freedom.

The next step is to focus on what you have, not on what you lack. Look around the world at the people who are so much less fortunate than you. Do you really have to go to a third world country to feel that you are fortunate? God has blessed you with many things. Until you are able to be thankful for those things and handle your current blessings, He can't bless you with greater things. Focus on what you have today and build on that because that is your foundation. That is your starting point, tell yourself today is the day that I am going to make it. Today I am going to be greater than yesterday and the day before.

If you focus all your energy on what you don't have, then you will always be a dreamer and never an achiever. There are people on this earth who watch things happen and people who make things happen. Which one are you?

The next thing is if you ask for nothing, you get nothing. You need to put it out there. What do you want? What are your expectations? What are your desires? Have a conversation with the Almighty God; then put what you want in writing. Your next step is to make it visible, have it where you can see it every day, and where you can have access to it. This is your reminder to keep focused on what you want and what you are going after.

You have conceived a thought of what you want your life to be like, and then you put it into action by being an achiever. You work toward your goals no matter how many challenges, road blocks, and obstacles come your way. No matter how many people tell you "No!" along the way or that you will not make it, you still push forward. You ask the Lord for strength, wisdom, and knowledge, and He will give you the desires of your heart.

On One Accord

Life is much like music; it does not matter if you are composing a classical master piece, country song, jazz, rock, pop, or R& B melody, the outcome is still the same. You are looking for certain tones, balances, and harmony in each of the different kinds of music. In life, it is vital that all aspects of your life are on one accord and every area of your life is balanced, so be in tune with your life. Know what is going on with you and around you. Once you are in tune with yourself, you will see more clearly how to proceed with your life. Some people just live their life from day to day and have no clue what they want to do or where they are going.

Harmony is an agreement in feeling, approach, and sympathy. It is the pleasing interaction between what you think, feel, say, and do. Having harmony in your life balances where you are today and where you want to go in the future. It becomes necessary when you are dealing with obstacles, hurdles, and turmoil in your life.

Life is a fine art, a painting, a musical masterpiece – it is a skill we develop only through living, through exploring new avenues, expanding our understanding, and creating the patterns that makes us extraordinary. How are you creating your masterpiece? Are you living your best life? It's time to rewrite your masterpiece and put your life back on track. Answer the following questions to start or recommit to your journey.

1. How can I be more in tune with my life?

   _____
   _____
   _____
   _____

2. What areas of my life are out of balance? What am I neglecting? What am I paying too much attention to? How can I refocus and get my life back in balance?

   _____
   _____
   _____
   _____

3. Do I have true Harmony in my life? If not, what can I do to get it? How important is it for me to have?

   _____
   _____
   _____
   _____

How do you See Yourself

In order to overcome challenges in your life, you have to be in sync with yourself and acknowledge this is the way that God has made you. It is important to know your strengths and weaknesses; you can build on your strengths and work on your weaknesses on a daily basis. Below is a list of words. Identify three strengths and three weaknesses, and then make it a point to work on them on a daily basis. It is your personal goal to be better every day:

professional	perfectionist	supportive
compassionate	patient	creative
honest	reliable	dependent
courageous	shy	sensitive
stubborn	risk-taker	dependable
loyal	steadfast	introvert
extrovert	dominant	passive
practical	logical	reasonable
controller	sincere	organizer
committed	faithful	poised
apathetic	empowered	talker

spontaneous	communicator	listener
determined	convincing	inspiring
sociable	optimistic	responsible

Bringing It Home

1. Self-confidence is Believing in Yourself when Others Don't

Self-confidence is an attitude which allows individuals to have positive, yet realistic views of themselves and their situations. Self-confident people trust their own abilities, have a general sense of control in their lives, and believe that, within reason, they will be able to do what they wish, plan, and expect. Having self-confidence does not mean that individuals will be able to do everything, but they have the confidence to do something. Self-confident people have expectations that are realistic. Even when some of their expectations are not met, they continue to be positive and accept themselves. They are not afraid of failing because they believe in their mind, body, and soul no matter how many times they fail. They will succeed. In their thought life, they can envision themselves succeeding.

2. What is your Motivation?

Motivation starts with the desire to be free, to be free from dependency on others, freedom to live the lifestyle we dream of, freedom to explore our ideas. Total freedom is not possible or desirable, but the struggle to achieve that ideal is the basis for motivation.

Ask any person who is successful in whatever he or she is doing what motivates him/her, and very likely the answer will be "goals." Goal Setting is extremely important to motivation and success. So what motivates you? Do you want to get a new job? Do you want a bigger house? Do you want to be self-employed? Do you want more money in the bank? The key questions are: What is your motivation and why do you do what you do?

3. Structure
Through discipline and structure comes self-discipline. Structure does not need to be suffocating and overwhelming. There is always room for creativity and self-expression within the confines of structure. Structure is not in-and-of-itself punitive, but rather, it creates a safe and predictable environment in which to operate. The reality of the matter is that when environments are safe, predictable, and structured, healthy growth, development, exploration, creativity, and innovation are on the horizon. Many times, we lose the battle because we lack structure in our lives. Would you jump in your car and drive without having a destination in mind? That would just not make sense. You need to start having a purpose and setting up a sound structure to fulfill that purpose.

Thoughts

Remember when you thought the roof was caving in on you? When you felt like the whole world was against you, but that voice in your head kept telling you, "Hang tough, you can do it." That was your inner strength. We all have it, and we draw on it when we need it the most. Listen to that voice of reason, that inner voice of strength telling you that no matter what the problem is you will succeed.

When facing problems, it is important to focus on the solution rather than the problem. The problem is already there. You cannot do anything about the problem; you cannot go back in time and change it. However, you can focus your energy on the solution, figure out how you are going to get out of the situation, overcome it, or get through it. Mentally, this will be time well spent because you are being active in overcoming your trials and tribulations.

Get-It-Together

It is almost impossible to realistically solve every problem in your life, at least all at one time. Think of a forest that is filled with trees and the trees represent your problems. Well, you are the lumber jack with a sharp axe ready to start chopping them down one by one. Within the next 24 hours, I want you to think of your forest. Don't focus on it too hard, but acknowledge that there is a problem. Your job is to focus on the solution to that problem and work toward solving it. What happens if you are not successful in your first attempt at solving your problem? That is okay! It just means that you have to get creative, be determined and resilient in getting the solution. Sometimes, you may have to come up with a different solution to the same problem.

Passion

Pouring Your Heat and Soul into Your Labor

Without passion man is a mere latent force and possibility, like the flint which awaits the shock of the iron before it can give forth its spark.

-Henri Frederic Amiel

Great ambition is the passion of a great character. Those endowed with it may perform very good or very bad acts. All depends on the principles which direct them.

-Napoleon Bonaparte

Earl Woods passed on his deep passion for golf to his son; his other gift was passing on the joy. As driven as Tiger Woods is to win, his joy of the competition equally shines through. Since the age of three, Tiger has been swinging a golf club; through the years he has perfected his swing so much so that it has brought him championships, wealth, joy, and passion for the game.

"I love to play golf, and that's my arena. And you can characterize it and describe it however you want, but I have a love and a passion for getting that ball in the hole and beating those guys."-Tiger Woods

Since Woods' PGA debut in 1996, he has dominated and reinvented the golf world. His passion for the game and willingness to work hard has paid off tremendously. He claimed the world's No. 1 ranking at age 21, eight years younger than anyone that had done it before (the previous youngest No. 1 was 29-year-old Bernhard Langer in 1986). Since turning pro, he has won 75 tournaments, 55 of those on the PGA tour.

Among his achievements, Woods has held the number one position in the world rankings for the most consecutive weeks and for the greatest total number of weeks. He has been awarded PGA Tour Player of the Year for a record eight times, and he has led the money list seven times (one behind Jack Nicklaus' record). Like Woods, if you live in your passion and do what you love to do you could be great at it. Oprah Winfrey says, "When you follow your passion, great things happen." Tiger Woods is a true testament of that statement.

My passion is what drives me to do what I do and be the best at it. I have great success in building businesses, motivating people, getting things done, and some great failures in trying. A lot of the time my failure fuels my passion. It is when I fail that I am tested, but I get back up, dust myself off, and do it again. My passion allows for mistakes, my passion allows me to forgive myself and it is a teaching tool.

Too often, people fail to make the distinction between being interested in a field, career, and profession or being called to do a service and loving what you do. To identify your passion, it is absolutely critical to discover if you truly enjoy the work, not just the topic, issue, or field.

If you want to find your passion, you *must* first *do* the work. If you are planning to buy a new car, you would set aside money a little at a time to make that dream a reality. Similarly, you would start researching different cars and test driving them. You would go to different dealers to get the best price; you would try to leave little doubt. Isn't your life's work entitled to at least that much consideration and preplanning? If this is your passion, you would want to know everything possible about it because it intrigues you, drives you, and motivates you.

Your passion does not usually appear overnight. It has been dwelling inside you for a long time. As a child, what were you passionate about? As a teenager, what were you passionate about? As a young adult, what were you passionate about? Often times, you will identify a pattern in what you are passionate about. It is up to you to identify what it is and go after it.

People who are passionate about their work do a better job. Since they care so much about the work, they don't settle for anything less than their best. They don't ever "just go through the motions." They pour all their thoughts and energy into doing the job well. Passionate people get more done. They don't spend time worrying about what they have to do next. They don't scheme to figure out how to get out of doing something. They focus on the solution rather than the problem. They are better equipped to improvise, adapt, and overcome situations related to their work.

I teach a graduate business class, and I asked my students how many of them actually work a full eight-hour day for their employer. Not one of them raised their hands; the average answer was they worked about five hours out of the eight-hour day. They were not passionate about their current job or with their employer. As a result, the employer is not getting total commitment.

When you feel passion for your job or your career, it shows. Regardless of what you do, it's how you do it that really matters. When you're passionate about what you're doing, it's infectious and gives off a high level of energy and enthusiasm. It may even rub off on those around you and create a better perception of you in their eyes. I've had people love me and hate me. While I prefer the love by a wide margin, I kind of prefer either to indifference because I'm not about making indifference; I'm about making a difference.

Tapping into Your Passion

What gets you excited? What is it that gets your mojo flowing in such a way that you just can't stop? Sometimes, it's hard to identify your passion because you love so many things, but because you love them doesn't necessarily mean that you are passionate about them. List some "what I love" thoughts that could spark your creativity and make your passion come alive. Think of five things that you are most passionate about to get your mojo flowing:

1._____

2._____

3._____

4._____

5._____

Take a good look at the five things you wrote down. Obviously, you love all five of them, but there is one that jumps out at you for some reason. The one you keep staring at and can't get out of your mind is the one you are most passionate about. God has a way of putting things right in front of our face even when we don't even realize it.

Turn your Passion into Profit

When turning your passion into profit, you have to be careful and work smarter, not harder. You will run into a lot of obstacles and need to face your fears, as things probably won't go as smoothly as you'd like them to go. It's all a part of the journey. However, none of it really matters when you love what you do. Some strategies to consider are working part-time in the field of interest, developing a partnership, and seeking out a mentor to help guide you to success.

Before you dive on into a new business, I suggest that you gain an insider's perspective by working part-time (even if only on a short term basis) in your field of interest before you commit to starting a business. You'll learn first-hand what's involved in running the type of business that you are interested in. It's a great way to get your feet wet; this experience can only improve your chances for success.

Secondly, I implore you to consider a partnership with someone who's passionate about the business end of your business. That way, you'll be able to spend more of your time doing what you love. If you decide to partner, be sure to choose your partner carefully and define clear expectations in the beginning. Having clear expectations keeps everyone on the same page of the mission and vision of the business.

Finally, seek out a mentor who has worked in your field of interest for a while. Ask them about the pros and cons, what's worked, and what hasn't. Direct competitors may be reluctant to talk with you for obvious reasons. You can avoid this dilemma by seeking the advice of business owners in other market areas.

Everyone wants to make a living doing what they love, but very few are ready to put in the effort required to make it happen. For me, this means setting goals that are specific, realistic, and deadline-based. The first step towards turning passion into profit is to get clear about what you want. Once you have identified what you love to do that is your passion, doing it every day is the easy part. Someone finding value in it and paying top dollar for your skills is the fun part. So perfect your craft and enjoy what you do; then people will find value in what you do and seek you. You see, you are in charge of your life. You are responsible for how your life looks today and what your future will look like.

Bringing It Home

1. Discovering your Passion
Most people are passionate about something but have suppressed their feelings for a number of reasons. You will want to discover what you are passionate about so you can find your position in life that will allow you to feel fulfilled. Your passions are always with you, yet you probably do not recognize or understand them. You will know you are passionate about something when you become naturally excited just thinking about it and even more excited when doing it.

2. Find your Passion by Looking in the Mirror
How many people do you know spend a significant amount of time wishing they were somewhere else instead of work? Despite their talent or intelligence, they're rarely successful because they're not tapping into their creative energies. Most people would agree that our passions frequently reveal themselves early in life, but until we look in the mirror and decide to make that change, nothing happens. For most of us, our actual calling requires more time to manifest because we are either soul-searching or waiting out of fear. The potential may be present, but how it should be nurtured isn't always clear. Take that deep look into the mirror and search your soul to find your hidden passion.

3. Your Passion is your Love
When you have a passion for your work, you find yourself loving what you do. You start dreaming and chasing that dream. However, do not chase it too fast and forget to enjoy what's going on right now in your life. When you stop looking at your passion as "work" and looking at it as something you love, you have truly found your calling!

Thoughts

Being passionate about something is more than the old saying "do what you love." It's looking forward to doing it without reservation. It is time flying by when you're doing it. It's working past quitting time, not because you're swamped with work, but because you were so intent you didn't notice the time. When you are passionate about what you do for a living, you enjoy it more. You also do it better.

You only live once so why not live your life doing what you love to do? Don't do it for the money, don't do it for the fame, don't do it for the accolades, do it because you love what you are doing and the people you are impacting.

Get-It-Together

Why waste time doing something if your heart isn't in it? Stop going through the motions and start living in your passion. Your challenge is to identify your passion in the next 72 hours and start doing something in your passion. Whatever your passion is, you have to buy a book to increase knowledge, rent a movie about it, research the Internet, volunteer or find a mentor to guide you in that area. But your challenge is to start doing something in your passion once you have identified it.

Commitment

It Separates the Haves from the Have Not's

Individual commitment to a group effort -- that is what makes a team work, a company work, a society work, a civilization work.

-Vince Lombardi

The single, most important factor in individual success is Commitment. Commitment ignites action. To commit is to pledge yourself to a certain purpose or line of conduct. It also means consistently practicing your beliefs. There are, therefore, two fundamental conditions for commitment. The first is having a sound set of beliefs. There is an old saying that goes, "Stand for something or you'll fall for anything." The second is faithful adherence to those beliefs with your behavior. Possibly the best description of commitment is "persistence with a purpose."

"Stand for something or you'll fall for anything." What is it in life that you stand for? This is a loaded question because we often think of self-first. If you do, then I challenge you to think bigger. Find something bigger than you and commit to it. Once you find that special thing that you stand for, people will challenge you, but that's okay because you believe in it and yourself. You will not listen to the nay-sayers and rhetoric; you will support your beliefs at all cost because you are committed.

You will develop faithful adherence to your beliefs and have "persistence with a purpose." Undoubtedly, there will be times when you will fall down, but you will have the fortitude to get back up and fight for what you believe in. You can lose all your money, you can lose your car, you can lose your house, you can lose a family member, but if you stay strong and steadfast, you can get it all back.

Commitment is responsibility. Most of us are committed to relationships, careers, or whatever through some level of fear. We fear that if we do not commit to our careers or relationships, we may lose them. But do these choices bring us joy, harmony, and love? Is our commitment strictly out of obligation because that is what we are choosing at the time? It is commendable to be responsible and committed at the same time, but do not lose yourself in the process.

How do we discern being committed to one's self verses to another's dream, direction, hopes, and desires? Sometimes, we feel that if we commit to another person or thing, that will suffice and we have done our part. We feel that through their accomplishments or progress, we may live vicariously through their experience. We feel that our only responsibility is to their success, not our own. Sadly, you cannot live through someone else's life; you can cheer them on, support them, and be happy for them. However, their life is not your life, and you have to start living yours.

Commitment to one's self takes enormous courage and self-discipline. First, you need to decide what it is you want to commit to. As mere mortals, we waiver in our self-discipline to stay committed to things, projects, or events. In addition, we inevitably allow other people to sabotage our commitment to ourselves. This is a back door that we create to disallow from staying committed to ourselves. Change occurs when you make up in your mind that you will be steadfast and have the endurance to go the distance and stay committed.

Commitment is most difficult and most readily proven during tough times. How someone weathers the storms of their life most clearly demonstrates their basic beliefs. It shows true character. Will you tuck your tail between your legs and run at the first sign of danger, or will you stand and fight for what you believe in?

January 1 every year, I see people making new resolutions and personal commitments to what they want to do for the next year. The number one resolution is losing weight and going to the gym. During the first four weeks of the New Year, you can't find an empty treadmill at the gym. But what happens after February when you don't see those same committed people any longer? Because some people don't see the results they were expecting, they quit. Some lose interest in the idea of getting that beach body because it is too hard and painful. Some lack the determination and motivation to achieve their goal.

Contrary to what many people think, commitment is hard and painful. Commitment takes every ounce of determination and motivation that you can muster up to be successful. When you put in the time, the effort, the blood, sweat and tears and stay on the path less traveled, you will see the fruits of your labor.

True Commitment

True commitment is tested when you have failed, not just once but several times, and your faith is also tested. Put failure in the right perspective because it's an opportunity for regrouping and evaluation while accepting the experience as part of the journey of success. Failure is not only the output of an unsuccessful activity; it is also the input of a successful one. Performance only changes and improves to the degree that you change and improve.

True commitment comes when you have the stamina to recover from a disaster and look at that situation in a different light. Your commitment does not come from the situation, but it comes from the outcome and what lies ahead. You believe in your heart that there are better days ahead and know that there is some better in store for you because this is God's promises to you. You are committed because of your strong faith in God.

True commitment is dedication to a particular organization, cause, or belief, and a willingness to get involved. People who are committed to an organization or effort truly believe that it is important, and they show up, follow through, and stick with it. If you are committed to an effort for a period of time, you will learn what you need to know to be more effective. You need time to try things out, make mistakes, and figure out a strategy that works.

If you've been putting off anything in your life, I invite you to ask yourself why. What are you waiting for? There will always be a new problem standing in your way. I urge you to fully commit yourself to a task or project and see it through to the end. As William James once proclaimed, "To change one's life: Start immediately. Do it flamboyantly. No exceptions."

What Am I Committed To

David McNally commented, "Commitment is the enemy of resistance, for it is the serious promise to press on, to get up, no matter how many times you are knocked down." If you want to realize what is real in your life, you must recognize what you are committed to.
People are motivated to be committed to different things. Where do you fall?

❏ I am committed to my family.

❏ I am committed to making money.

❏ I am committed to my health.

❏ I am committed to my career.

❏ I am committed to greed.

❏ I am committed to materialistic possession.

❏ I am committed to my relationship.

❏ I am committed to improving my life.

- ❏ I am committed to myself.

- ❏ I am committed to God.

It's time to get real and be honest with yourself. What areas of your life are you committed to and what areas do you need to be committed to in order to be a better person? Commitment is the ability to stand fast when others fall as well as bounce back when you have failed or been defeated. This is when your true character shows up and you know what you are made of.

Bringing It Home

1. Commitment to Self
You often hear self-preservation is number one. Does that apply if you are a mother or a father? Do you then put your children's needs before your own; is their life more important than yours? You have a commitment to yourself first. If you are not able to take care of you first, then you are not equipped to take care of anyone else. You have a commitment to yourself to be physically, spiritually, and financially stable. You don't owe it to anyone else. You owe it to yourself. You have been given gifts and talents by God, and you just have to figure out how to use them.

2. Commitment to God
Do not be fooled by those who think they know everything. A person who thinks they know

everything is often a fool because they think they can learn nothing. Listen to your inner self and hear God's words and see His vision for your life. The LORD wants your conviction to be strong. He wants your foundation to be powerful, and your faith to be everlasting. You are to be deeply rooted in the word, in the Spirit, and in the presence and the knowledge of God. Genesis 26:12 says, "Isaac planted crops in that land and the same year reaped a hundredfold, because the LORD blessed him." You do your part and allow the LORD to do His.

3. Commitment to Others
You will get far in this life once you realize that it's not about you. Your destiny and your purpose for being on this earth is a divine plan. You were put here for a greater purpose, to serve in some capacity. Once you have mastered that idea, that concept, that notion, that simple truth, you are well on your way to true greatness. Commitment is a two-way street. You only get it if you are willing to give it.

Thoughts

Staying committed to one's self is the most courageous human experience. Courage is choosing to be better tomorrow than you are today. The human experience is very simple. It is about personal growth. We either set it up for ourselves through our own personal commitment or life will present it to us, sometimes in a form that does not feel very good.

I encourage you to stay in the game, learn the rules, and be resilient. Being totally committed will bring you self-satisfaction at the end of the day. Just stay the course and do not let fear or uncertainty control you. By staying committed, you might just surprise yourself.

Get-It-Together

Over the next several days is your time to get real and get committed. Earlier in the chapter, you were asked what you were committed to. I challenge you to increase your commitment on your road to greatness. What three things are you going to be committed to in addition to what you are already committed to? You have 48 hours to decide and become dedicated to your new commitments. They don't have to be three huge monumental things, but they need to be significant in your life. Whatever they are, Finish them!

Vision

If You Can See It, You can Achieve it

When I dare to be powerful, to use my strength in the service of my vision, then it becomes less and less important whether I am afraid.

-Audre Lorde

Sam Walton, founder of Wal-Mart, graduated from the University of Missouri in 1940 and got a job at J.C. Penny's as a management trainee. It was at Penney's that Sam Walton began to learn about retail, and his vision began to grow. Walton knew that he had to develop any good idea with persistence, excellence, and a willingness to succeed.

Sam Walton's first store was a franchise of the Butler Brothers. Walton was successful in making his first store profitable by using the same strategies he used in his Wal-Mart stores:

1. Location means everything - Walton located his stores in places that were accessible to people who lived in the area.
2. Identify with your customer - Walton made sure that his shelves were stocked with popular items that people wanted and needed.
3. Keep it Low – Walton kept his prices down by buying his merchandise at wholesale prices.
4. Something different – Walton's stores were open for longer hours; more than his competitors.

Sam Walton went on to open "Walton's 5 & 10" stores and became very successful. However, his vision increased with his success. He opened his first Wal-Mart store in 1962 in Rogers, Arkansas, and never looked back. Wal-Mart stores boast over $300 billion a year in sales and more than 3,800 stores in the United States while employing over 1.5 million people.

Sam Walton is a man who had a great vision and made that vision a reality, thus affecting the lives of many people, the people who are employed and the people who use Wal-Mart products on an everyday basis.

Visions generally have more clarity than dreams; they are often vivid and lucid. Seeing your outcome in your visions is not a hard thing to do. However, making your vision a reality is a far greater challenge than just seeing the vision. Some people may go their entire life and never envision what their life should be like. Then, there are those who have the ability to envision their life but never act upon it. They lie in a dormant state of complacency for years.

The gap between how we are and how we could be is what provides the momentum and the challenge to respond. Many great leaders understand this concept, and this is what makes them successful. Great leaders envision their future; they look at the possibility of what could be and not what is. Those with great vision act with purpose because they know something greater is waiting down the road, and they can't wait to get there.

There are many great leaders that we can learn from who had powerful visions that ultimately came to pass. Ben Franklin was as much the founder of modern America as was

Washington and Jefferson and the others of our Founding Fathers. Franklin was principled but tolerant, secular but reverential, a pioneer scientist, a practical entrepreneur, a political activist, with a firm commitment to self-improvement and social betterment. He was a person of virtue, a promoter of values. Franklin was also the visionary of an ethical society as an important contributor to the moral health of a nation. However, we are living in a nation where it is tough to uphold Ben Franklin's vision. It is up to you as an individual to make a change, to make an impact, to make yourself better, to make your family better, your community better, and our nation better.

Another great leader of our times was Dr. Martin Luther King, Jr. He knew that it wasn't enough just to talk the talk, that he had to walk the walk for his words to be credible. Dr. King was a man who put his life on the line for freedom and justice every day, the man who braved threats and jail and beatings and who ultimately paid the highest price to make democracy a reality for all Americans.

Dr. King's great dream of a vibrant, multiracial nation united us in justice, peace, and reconciliation; a nation that has a place at the table for children of every race and room at the inn for every needy child. Dr. King was an amazing leader and visionary who embraced the unity of all faiths in love and truth. You see what the vision of one man can do? What about your vision? Ask yourself how powerful is your vision and how far will your vision take you?

Paying the Price for Your Vision

There are times in life we look at what others have and we get jealous, become envious, and want it for ourselves. However, you don't know what that person did to get those things, and more importantly, are you willing to pay the price to get it yourself? In order to get the things that other people have, you have to be willing to do the things that they have done. It is okay to look at what someone else has done and say that you wish you could accomplish that level of success but make it your own vision.

Most people want to have an amazing job and financial independence, but not everyone is willing to suffer through 60-hour workweeks, long commutes, insufferable paperwork, to navigate uninformed corporate hierarchies and the confines of an infinite cubicle misery. People want to be rich without the risk or the delayed gratification necessary to accumulate wealth. If your vision is to be rich or wealthy, what are you willing to risk in order to achieve your goal?

I would also venture to say that most people want to have great sex and a tremendous relationship, just like we see on television but not everyone is willing to go through the tough communication, the awkward silences, the hurt feelings, and the emotional breakdowns to get there. Everyone is not willing to invest in his or her relationship spiritually, emotionally, physically, and financially to get the paid dividends on the backside.

"Nothing good in life comes easy;" I know you have been told that a hundred times before. The good things in life we accomplish are defined by where we enjoy the suffering, where we enjoy the struggle. You truly appreciate the things you acquire more through the pain it took to get there.

I think Mark Manson said it best, "If you want the benefits of something in life, you have to also want the costs. If you want the six-pack, you have to want the sweat, the soreness, the early mornings, and the hunger pangs. If you want the yacht, you have to also want the late nights, the risky business moves, and the possibility of pissing off a person or ten." "If you find yourself wanting something month after month, year after year, yet nothing happens and you never come any closer to it, then maybe what you actually want is a fantasy, an idealization, an image, and a false promise. Maybe you don't actually want it at all."

No matter what your vision may be rest assured that it comes at a price that you have to be willing to pay. A fee to health, wealth, success, and prosperity; there are no short cuts to success.

Your Perception is Your Reality

If you can believe that you are going to be great, then it's going to be your reality that you will be great. Make up in your mind what you want for your life. If this is not the life that you had envisioned for yourself, then create a new vision. Your first step is to ask the Lord for a new anointing, for a fresh start, and create a new vision for your life. How you perceive your life to be will ultimately become your reality because you will start living your life according to what you believe. If your mind can conceive it, then you can achieve it. You are going to focus on five areas of your life that you envision being better than before. Then, write down key things you want to change or enhance in those areas of your life to have the best life ever:

Spiritual Life:

_____
_____
_____
_____
_____
_____

Relationships:

_____
_____
_____
_____
_____
_____

Finances:

_____
_____
_____
_____
_____
_____

Career and Work:

_____
_____
_____
_____
_____
_____

Physical Health:

_____
_____
_____
_____
_____
_____

Now that you have written down what you envision for life, it's time to go after it with full throttle. Nothing should hold you back or get in the way of your dreams. Claim what is rightfully yours, claim it in your mind, claim it in your heart, and claim it in your soul that this is your new life.

Bringing It Home

1. Owning Your Vision

When I go to a store and purchase a puzzle, I own it. It is mine to take home and assemble it perfectly. Well, it the same with your visions. You are in complete control of your thoughts and your visions. What you should do is take the time to perfect your craft. Envisioning yourself doing it is just one-fourth of the battle. Now, you have to finish, follow through, and perfect your craft.

2. Practice Your Vision

Whatever you see yourself doing, you have to practice it daily to be the best at it. Have the attitude that no one can do it like you. Believe it or not, you are unique, and I can prove it to you. Just look at your fingertip. I guarantee there is no one else on God's green earth with the same finger tips like yours, which makes you unique. Your fingerprint is one of a kind, and no one else has a print like yours. So, bring your "A" game every time and see yourself succeeding.

3. Your Vision is More than You

True vision is eternal. It goes beyond what one man or woman could achieve solely. It has genuine and pure substance and does more than include other people; it adds value to them. You must never forget that you were not put on this earth to be selfish, self-centered, or self-seeking. You were created for a greater purpose to help others, and your vision should be focused on serving other people. If your vision

[133]

does not reflect helping others, then it's probably too narrow.

Thoughts

Happiness is something you decide on ahead of time. Whether I like my room or not doesn't depend on the furniture I have or how it is arranged; it is how I arrange it in my mind. It is all based on perception. Your perception is your reality. If you think and believe that you have a wonderful life, then you will life a great life. Don't limit your vision for your life, think the impossible, pray for what you think is the unattainable, but believe in yourself that it is achievable. No matter what anybody else says, reach for your STARS!

Get-It-Together

Over the next several days, take some time and do some reflection over your life. Look at where you have been, where are today, and where you want to go in the future. Before you do anything else, pray and ask God for guidance for your future. Then, write down a vision statement for your life. Just like most major companies have a mission and vision statement, so should you. This vision statement will allow you to define what your successful life should look like. It is important to include dates and give yourself a target to aim for. Success is more likely when you are more specific about what you want in detail, and you hold yourself accountable by setting deadlines.

Destiny

What You were Created to Do

Destiny knocks at the door, courage answers it.

-Dr. Donavan L. Outten

Successful and unsuccessful people do not vary greatly in their abilities. They vary in their desires to reach their potential.

-John Maxwell

What is destiny and how does it impact your life? Destiny is regarded by some as fate, a fixed timeline of events that is inevitable and unchangeable, and the future knowable thorough means of predication. This has led to an assumption of predication as fortune-telling though the actual practice accounts for self-determination of individual people and an unknowable future.

Others believe that they choose their own destiny by choosing different paths throughout their life and that they can alter their destiny by the choices they make through everyday living. Some people believe they were destined to be great, destined to be wealthy, or destined to have a terrible life.

In any case, destiny can be referred to as a predetermined course of events. It may be conceived as a predetermined future, whether in general or of an individual. What you perceive your future to be will come to pass if you work for it, believe in it, and live your life towards it.

What you have today does not reflect what you will obtain tomorrow. If you have the capability of looking into your future and seeing what lies ahead, then all you have to do is work towards your goal.

Walking towards your destiny is no easy task because you will have obstacles and hurdles along the way. There will be road blocks that will make you think that you are going down the wrong path, but you will need to have patience, endurance, and faith. Your faith will play a big part in finding and fulfilling your destiny; you will need to seek guidance from God. If you go at this alone, you will surely fail. Finding and fulfilling your destiny is a life long journey, and you need the help and support of others but mostly guidance from God.

God is the creator of all things; He is the alpha and omega. He knows our beginning and our ending. Understand that your road map was perfectly designed by God; it's how you implement that road map that matters. If it is your belief that God has something greater for you and that you are destined for it, then you will have it.

Live your life and walk in your destiny. Don't wait for someone to give it to you; instead, go after it. You only live once, so live a life without regret. Don't worry about failure because failure is a tool preparing you for life's hard lessons. When you start walking in your destiny, you won't worry about fear and failure. You will see them in a different light. You will use them to your advantage and success.

If you are a dreamer and never an achiever, you will never have anything but dreams. If you are a person who watches things happen and never makes things happen, you will never accomplish anything. You must believe that your dreams and destiny are right before your feet. Acknowledge God and He will reveal it to you.

Deuteronomy 30:5 affirms God's commitment: "He will bring you to the land that belonged to your fathers, and you will take possession of it. He will make you more prosperous and numerous than your fathers." Take back what is rightfully yours and claim your victory. Once you understand who you are in Christ, hell won't be able to keep you from your destiny!

Destiny's Ripple Effect

For every action, there is a reaction. Most people would agree with that statement. Then, there is the cause and effect theory. Because this happened, then the outcome of the situation was that. Let me give you an example: picture yourself throwing a rock into a pond. What happens to the water in the pond? The water begins to ripple once the rock hits it. The energy from the rock sends shock waves and the waves of energy continue to flow. Your life is similar in comparison. What you should do is throw your rock at life, but in a positive way. Once that rock hits, you are then sending positive waves of energy to people around you, your thoughts, your ideas, your goals, your dreams, and toward your destiny. So, for every action, there is a reaction. Your action is throwing positive energy out, and the reaction is positive events unfolding in your life.

You want to produce positive waves of energy throughout your life, and living a positive life is living a more fulfilling life. What you do in life truly affects someone else. How you make that impact on them is entirely up to you. What you send out to the universe does come back to you in some shape, form, or fashion. The universe will pay you back with kindness, or it could pay you back with grief. The ripple will continue to flow throughout your life; the more positive rocks you throw at life, the more positive things you get back in return.

Destiny is tied to Effort

Just because you are destined to be great does not mean it's going to happen without you putting forth effort. Great people just don't wake up in the morning and have everything handed to them on a silver platter. God promised you greatness, but you have to put in the work to obtain that greatness. Michael Phelps, the most decorated Olympian of all time with 22 medals, did not get that title by accident.

Born on June 30, 1985, in Baltimore, Maryland, Michael Phelps competed in his first Olympics at the age of 15, as part of the U.S. men's swim team. He went on to win medals at the Olympic Summer Games in Athens, Beijing, and London, accumulating a total of 22 medals—18 gold, two silver and two bronze—and setting the record for the most medal wins of any Olympic athlete.

Phelps launched his swimming career at the Loyola High School pool. He met his coach, Bob Bowman, when he started training at the North Baltimore Aquatic Club at the Meadowbrook

Aquatic and Fitness Center. The coach immediately recognized Phelps's talents and fierce sense of competition and began an intense training regime. By 1999, Phelps had made the U.S. National B Team.

At the age of 15, Phelps became the youngest American male swimmer at an Olympic Games in 68 years. While he didn't win a medal at the 2000 Summer Olympics in Sydney, Australia, he would soon become a major force in competitive swimming. He dedicated time, energy, and effort to his craft to become the best in the world.

Bill Gates began to show an interest in computer programming at age 13. Through technological innovation, keen business strategy, and aggressive business tactics, he and partner Paul Allen built the world's largest software business, Microsoft. In the process, Gates became one of the richest men in the world.

Gates enrolled at Harvard University, originally thinking of a career in law. But his freshman year saw him spend more of his time in the computer lab than in class. Gates did not really have a study regimen. Instead, he could get by on a few hours of sleep, cram for a test, and pass with a reasonable grade. He took a chance on his passion and left school to start his own business.

Gates's acumen for not only software development but also business operations put him in the position of leading the company and working as its spokesperson. While Gates was destined for greatness, he had to work extremely hard for it and make his own dream a reality. The fruits of his labor can be seen in many households and businesses across the world. Do you have the courage to go after your dreams and fulfill your destiny?

Bringing It Home

1. Road Blocks to your Destiny
"*Momma said there'd be days like this.*" Anytime you are on the road to your destiny, you can be sure that you will face some road blocks. Some road blocks you will be able to simply go around. Others, you will be able to follow a detour. However, there are some road blocks that are so enormous that you have to re-evaluate your situation. Don't be dismayed because a road block doesn't mean that you are not going to get to your destiny. It just means that you are just going to have to wait a little longer. You have been delayed, but you have not been denied. Sometimes, those delays are a blessing in disguise because maybe you were not ready and had to complete something before moving ahead. Take that road block as an opportunity to re-evaluate and assess your situation, then move ahead.

2. Destiny vs. Passion

Moving towards your destiny should also mean that you are moving toward what you are passionate about in life. You are fulfilling your destiny when you are working in your passion. What is it in life that you are passionate about? What makes you motivated, concerned, or inspired? Your destiny should follow your passion. Oftentimes, we neglect what is important to us in life and miss the big picture. With your passion, you must develop a strong sense of persistence. You need to develop a *"can't give up attitude."* Persistence is a byproduct of passion. If you see persistence, passion is at work.

3. *Believe what God has for you*

Your destiny is right before your feet. Acknowledge God and He will reveal it to you. Deuteronomy 30:5 says, **"**He will bring you to the land that belonged to your fathers, and you will take possession of it. He will make you more prosperous and numerous than your fathers." Take back what is rightfully yours and claim your victory. Once you understand who you are in Christ, hell won't be able to keep you from your destiny!

Thoughts

Destiny is not something to be waited for; it is something to be achieved. If you want to live a certain kind of life, you are going to have to be proactive so you can consciously create the life that you want. You must first mentally visualize and then physically create what you want. You can do this by having a clear vision and developing strong intentions. Your life is your gift; how you appreciate it and use it is entirely up to you. Live your life today; believing what you have tomorrow is greater and better because that is your Destiny waiting on you.

Get-It-Together

This act is simple; create a vision board no matter how small or big and stick to it! You know what you want for your life and take the first step by putting it in the atmosphere and put it on a board where you can see it every day!

Gratitude

Developing A Spirit of Gratefulness

Gratitude is merely the secret hope of further favors.

-Francious de la Rochefoucauld

Gratitude is not only the greatest of virtues, but the parent of all the others.

-Cicero

Have you ever found yourself in the middle of a seemingly good day and suddenly you become aggravated by the slightest little thing? Maybe the 5:00 o'clock traffic on the road home was stalled, or dinner plans for the evening were disrupted. And that one little thing shifted your whole mindset into negativity!

The next time this happens, consider stopping yourself in the midst of the turmoil and opening your mind to all that you could be grateful for instead. Recognize all that you have: your friends, family, home, car, career, or just the chance God has given you to take in all that this beautiful day holds. Waking up each day is a blessing in itself because you have the opportunity to make a change in your life.

When you express gratitude for what you've been given, even if it is in the form of being grateful for a challenge, God hears your heart's joy and He responds in kind. When we are happy in our heart and soul, whatever we need flows to us by divine grace. To realize that you have been given much or have been spared by God's good grace is not a hard thing to do; all you have to do is turn on your television and watch the 11:00 o'clock news. Every night, the news is filled with devastation, destruction, pain, and heartache of other people's lives.

Someone has just been diagnosed with breast cancer. Someone's child has just been abducted, someone lost their life in a car accident today, someone just lost a son or daughter in the war, someone just lost their house, three thousand people just lost their jobs, someone just lost a limb in an accident, and someone lost a friend. You should be grateful because you survived today without losing something, and you were blessed because you were protected by God.

Whether you believe in God or not, ponder this: the world's major religions, including Christianity, Judaism, Islam, and Hindu, prize gratitude as a morally beneficial emotional state that encourages reciprocal kindness. Gratitude also encourages a positive cycle of reciprocal kindness among people since one act of gratitude encourages another.

Most people are so busy thinking about the next thing or their terrible past that they don't wake up and look around at their present moment, the here and now. They cannot live in the moment and enjoy life as they know it because they are not grateful. Gratitude is about waking up each morning and being grateful for what you have that day by recognizing and respecting what's around you.

Don't ever compare your life with someone else's because on the outside their life may look good, but you don't know what hell they may be going through on the inside. Sometimes, we can lose ourselves in wondering how we "measure up" to some standard set by someone else, the media, or our parents. The only measurements that really count are: Are you happy? Are you fulfilled? Are you satisfied?

On the whole, gratitude is the practice of consciously calling to mind, or listing out, the things you are thankful for. Whenever we express our thanks for something we have received, we are letting the universe know that we appreciate something. It is universal feedback. And the more we give thanks for something, the more likely it is that we will continue to receive more of that very same thing.

Recognizing Your God Moment

Ever had a moment when God seemed to "tap on your shoulder" and remind you that He is always there and always faithful? We all have "God moments" because they are of God. God is in them. God's breath is on our cheek. Time seems to stop or at least stand still for a profound moment. Even in the midst of the storm, God will come in and give you peace. I believe God comes at pivotal points in our life to let us know we are not walking alone. Personally I can distinctly remember several God moments when He showed up when I was at a low point in my life.

My last God moment was on my 40th birthday; I was feeling down about turning 40 and reflecting on my life and thinking that it was halfway over. I spent my birthday in the Turks & Caicos Islands and decided to go jet skiing; little did I know I was in for a treat. My tour guide, Philip, took me out in the most scenic crystal clear blue water, and my senses were on overload. As we drove out into the middle of the ocean, he took time for us to stop and admire the beauty that God created.

I was in awe of the creation that the Almighty God had created from the sky blue heavens to the crystal clear blue water. I jumped in the middle of the ocean and heard God speak to me that my life was a gift, and it was far from over. Be grateful for all that you have, be grateful for all that you have experienced, for the best is yet to come. I embraced that moment with God and a rush of gratification overcame me. I was released from worry over turning 40; I was released from worry about paying bills; I was released from worry about any sickness in my body, and I was released from worry about my career. I knew at that moment that I was in the hands of God and all would be perfectly divine.

What are your God moments? Reflect back to when you got a check in the mail unexpectedly and had no money in the bank. What about the time God kept you at home 15 minutes longer than you wanted to be only to find out there was a fatal car accident 15 minutes earlier on the same route you go to work? How about those late nights you were up sick and after your prayer, a peace came over you and your pain subsided? Only you can truly appreciate your God moments when it happens. Remember the moments you feel God's overwhelming grace and loving presence in your life; you need to recognize and respect it.

What am I Grateful For?

Do not go another day without realizing and acknowledging what you have in your life today and being grateful for it. If you can't appreciate what you currently have, why should God give you more? Luke16:10 says, "He who is faithful in a very little thing is faithful also in much; and he who is unrighteous in a very little thing is unrighteous also in much." Therefore if you have not been faithful in the use of unrighteous wealth, who will entrust the true riches to you?" This is a simple task, one that should take no time at all. Name 10 things in your life that you are grateful for:

1._____

2._____

3._____

4._____

5._____

6._____

7._____

8._____

9._____

10._____

Once you are able to appreciate what you have and are responsible with it, you will be able to handle the increase of blessings that God has in store for you.

Being Grateful and Giving Back

Giving back for most people is something more of a lifestyle, something they have always done. They are grateful for their lives no matter how rich or poor, they are grateful for what they have and willing to share with the world. When I think of the quote "To whom much is given much is require" two people come to mind and they are Oprah and Bono. Both are grateful of their successes and give back unselfishly.

Oprah Winfrey, born in Kosciusko, Mississippi, was reared by her grandmother on a farm where she "began her broadcasting career" by learning to read aloud and perform recitations at the age of three.

Oprah Winfrey's broadcasting career began at age 17, when she was hired by WVOL radio in Nashville and two years later, signed on with WTVF-TV in Nashville as a reporter/anchor.

In January 1984, she came to Chicago to host WLS-TV's "AM Chicago," a faltering local talk show. In less than a year, she turned "AM Chicago" into the hottest show in town. The format was soon expanded to one hour, and in September 1985, it was renamed "The Oprah Winfrey Show." Oprah Winfrey was named one of the 100 Most Influential People of the 20th Century by *Time* magazine and in 1998, received a Lifetime Achievement Award from the National Academy of Television Arts and Sciences.

She is one of the partners in Oxygen Media, Inc., a cable channel and interactive network presenting programming designed primarily for women. In 2000, Oprah's Angel Network began presenting a $100,000 "Use Your Life Award" to people who are using their lives to improve the lives of others.

Oprah Winfrey's dream of building a first-class school to nurture, educate, and turn gifted South African girls from impoverished backgrounds into the country's future leaders finally came true in 2007. Oprah has worked and obtained much in her life, but in return, she has given much back. It is her gratitude of the life that she has that grants her the opportunity to help others.

As lead singer in one of the most popular rock bands of all time, Irish-born guitarist Bono has become familiar to the general public as much for his support of social causes as for his trademark blue sunglasses and energetic performances as lead singer in the musical group U2. Bono went from wowing concert audiences with songs such as "Sunday, Bloody Sunday" during the 1980s to spearheading benefit tours during the 1990s to speaking about Africa's AIDS epidemic before a church congregation in Lincoln, Nebraska, in 2002.

Bono's resume includes an exhaustive section on social activism. In 1984, he appeared on Band Aid's charity recording "Do They Know It's Christmas?" After U2's historic Live Aid performance in 1985, Bono traveled to Ethiopia with his wife, Ali. They spent several weeks helping with an education and famine relief project. In 1986, U2 headlined Amnesty International's Conspiracy of Hope tour. Bono also performed at 1999's Net Aid, a concert broadcasted live over the Internet that raised money to relieve third-world debts. Since 1999, Bono has become increasingly involved in campaigning for third-world debt relief and raising awareness of the plight of Africa, including the AIDS pandemic.

Bono could have easily turned his head and enjoyed his fame and fortune, but he decided to make a difference because he was grateful and wanted to give back. People like Oprah and Bono are true humanitarians. They genuinely care about other people. When they are given something, they are compelled to help and share.

Bringing It Home

1. Being Grateful All the Time
Gratitude should be remembered every day of the year, not just during special times. Too often, during Thanksgiving and the holiday season we focus on being grateful. However, this view is short-sighted because we live in a world that revolves 365 days a year and should be

grateful for all days, not just selected days. After all, isn't giving thanks at all times really just reaffirming our trust in and love for God?

2. Gratitude Creates Peace
Your blessings will increase just by being grateful for what you have and not worrying about what is coming. This will also generate a vast amount of peace in your life because you are satisfied with what God has given you and will give you in the future.

3. Express Appreciation
Showing appreciation for something is as important a personal gesture today as it was a hundred years ago. When you can say "thank you" for a job well done or for an act of kindness, it is rather simple just to write a personalized thank you note to show appreciation.

Thoughts

Everything that you have today: your wealth, family, friends, health, and knowledge could be taken away in the blink of an eye. The Lord will give it to you, and just as easy, the Lord could take it away. It is so important to be humble and grateful for all that you have because if it was not for the Lord blessing you, you would not have what you have today.

The Lord just wants you to recognize Him and His blessings. If you do this, then you will receive more. If you are grateful for what you have and can handle it appropriately, He will bless you with more because you were responsible, humble, and grateful. Deuteronomy 12:7 says, "There, in the presence of the LORD your God, you and your families shall eat and shall rejoice in everything you have put your hands to, because the LORD your God has blessed you."

Get-It-Together

Being grateful is a way of life. It is waking up in the morning and thanking God for another day. I challenge you to change your lifestyle of being grateful and having an attitude of gratitude. The next time you are driving and someone cuts you off, I challenge you to thank God that you did not get into a car accident or curse the other driver. The next time you see an ambulance going by with its lights flashing, I challenge you to pray for the person who they are going for and thank God for your health. The next time you see a homeless person, you pray for their strength and a change in their situation, and then thank God that He spared you.

References:

John C. Maxwell, *Thinking For A Change* (New York, NY: Warner Books, 2005), 30.

R. K. Prabhu & U. R. Rao (1960) *"Mind of Mahatma Gandhi,"* Published by : Jitendra T. Desai Navajivan Mudranalaya, Ahemadabad-380014 India

About the Author

Dr. Donavan Outten is a powerful and energetic motivational speaker, entrepreneur and President of Educate U Foundation, an organization dedicated to helping to decrease the Achievement Gap in America. Dr. Outten is so dedicated to the cause of youth development that all proceeds from the sales of this book will go to research, training, program development and scholarships for minorities and underrepresented youth.

Dr. Outten has dedicated the last 20 years of his life to education. Most recently he has held administrator positions at Upper Iowa University and Unity College. Both domestically and internationally he gives inspirational lectures and keynote addresses at conferences, universities, churches, and community organizations. Dr. Outten is also the author of Skills for Success, a book dedicated to imparting the skills for living a life of success. Dr. Outten is led and moved by the spirit of God, and it shows through his work.

Made in the USA
San Bernardino, CA
30 May 2014